Rule of Law and Governance in the Palestinian Authority

DELIVERING BETTER POLICIES AND LEGISLATION FOR PEOPLE

Please cite this publication as:
OECD (2022), *Rule of Law and Governance in the Palestinian Authority: Delivering Better Policies and Legislation for People*, OECD Publishing, Paris, https://doi.org/10.1787/68ffa992-en.

ISBN 978-92-64-65136-4 (print)
ISBN 978-92-64-43099-0 (pdf)
ISBN 978-92-64-39987-7 (HTML)
ISBN 978-92-64-34024-4 (epub)

Photo credits: Cover © Yacoub Rabah/Shutterstock.com.

Corrigenda to publications may be found on line at: www.oecd.org/about/publishing/corrigenda.htm.

Foreword

As highlighted in the OECD Policy Framework on Sound Public Governance, effective policy and legislative development is critical to ensuring that governments can translate long-, medium- and short-term policy goals into concrete actions. It also provides an opportunity for governments to collaborate with a broad array of stakeholders and, as such, is core to the democratic process. It ensures that public governance values – such as integrity, openness and transparency, inclusiveness and accountability – are adopted widely across government, and mainstreamed across the policy cycle.

Rule of law and sound policy and legislative development are key objectives of the Palestinian Authority's (PA) ongoing efforts to build stronger institutions, address economic and societal challenges, and, ultimately, promote people's trust in the decision-making process. The *Basic Law* of 2002 outlines an institutional framework and mechanisms based on the rule of law, quality control and oversight of decision-making authorities. Moreover, the *Guidelines on Legislative Drafting* and *Guidelines on Secondary Legislative Drafting* were important early steps to institutionalise best practices in support of a transparent, evidence-based and people-centred legislative development process in the PA. Two OECD reports published in 2011 informed the Palestinian Authority's later efforts to review existing regulatory practices and update legislative drafting and public consultation guidelines.

Today, better law-making mechanisms and regulatory principles continue to be key features of the PA's strategic plans: Pillar 1 of the "National Policy Agenda 2017-22" notably cites the legislative process as a key priority. However, the *de facto* dissolution of the Palestinian Legislative Council (PLC) following the 2006 elections means law- and policy-making take place in a particularly challenging setting. To date, the PLC remains inactive and legislation is being issued by presidential decree. The PA also faces a number of other cross-cutting challenges that further hinder the Authority's efforts to reform the legislative- and policy-development processes: from humanitarian emergencies, fiscal deficits and high wage bills to specific governance challenges relating to ministries' weakened capacities for planning or the absence of institutional mechanisms to aptly co-ordinate legislative planning.

This Review looks at existing institutional frameworks, structures, mechanisms, and capacities to better address the aforementioned challenges hampering the policy and legislative process in the PA. Building on previous work, notably the 2017 assessment of the PA's legislative process by EUPOL COPPS, the Review draws on first-hand information collected from key institutions involved in these processes, as well as established OECD standards and good practices for sound policy and legislative development. It presents a detailed assessment of policy- and law-making in the PA and offers actionable recommendations to guide the Authority in administering requisite reforms.

While this Review focuses on the early stages of policy making, principally on legislation, a forthcoming complementary Review will look at other stages of the policy-making process, including policy delivery, monitoring and evaluation. In addition, the OECD supports the Authority through the development of *The Good Practices Manual for Policy and Regulatory Planning,* which aims to institutionalise clear guidelines for better planning and regulatory practices.

Both this Review and the forthcoming Manual are the result of the OECD's contribution to the "Support the Palestinian Authority to enhance Governance and the Rule of Law" project funded by the European Union. The project seeks to contribute to a more effective, transparent and participatory policy- and law-making process, and enhance people's and businesses' trust in the Authority's action. In line with the strategic priorities of the MENA-OECD Governance Programme under the OECD Public Governance Committee, the project deepens the OECD's support to the PA on issues of governance and the rule of law. Through the MENA-OECD Governance Programme, a strategic partnership between countries in the Middle East and North Africa (MENA) region and OECD Member countries, the OECD has supported the PA's efforts in several areas related to public governance, such as open government, integrity and anti-corruption, citizen participation, gender equality, budget management and local governance. The project is also implemented in close cooperation with the SIGMA Programme, a joint initiative of the OECD and the EU, principally financed by the EU.

This document was approved by the Public Governance Committee and Regulatory Policy Committee via written procedure on the 26th August 2022 and prepared for publication by the OECD Secretariat.

The views expressed herein can in no way be taken to reflect the official opinion of the Palestinian Authority.

Acknowledgements

The report was prepared by the OECD Public Governance Directorate (GOV) under the leadership of Elsa Pilichowski, Director. It was developed under the strategic direction of Martin Forst, Head of the Governance Reviews and Partnerships Division in GOV, and of Miriam Allam, Head of the MENA-OECD Governance Programme.

Sara Fyson, Jeroen Michels, and Johannes Klein (Part I), and Daniel Trnka, Richard Alcorn, and Yola Thürer (Part II) co-authored the report and were responsible for the data collection and analysis. Valuable feedback was received by Laura Völker, Andrea Uhrhammer, Camila Saffirio, Amira Tlili, Jean-Jacques Hible, Guillaume Biganzoli and Yusuf Ashmawy. Support in the data-collection and review was provided by Ra'id Malki and Nadia Abu Alia. Ciara Muller with the support of Francesca Romani prepared the manuscript for publication and controlled the quality.

This Review would not have been possible without the significant commitment and support of the Palestinian Prime Minister's Office. The authors are particularly thankful to Dr. Estephan Salameh, Advisor to the Prime Minister for Planning and Aid Coordination, for facilitating all exchanges between the OECD and different PA institutions in order to collect and verify data.

The authors also express their gratitude towards the following institutions for completing the OECD Questionnaires administered for the purpose of the review: the Prime Minister's Office (PMO); the General Secretariat of the Council of Ministers (GS); the Office of the President (OoP); the General Personnel Council (GPC); the Ministry of Justice (MoJ); the Advisory and Legislation Bureau (Diwan); the Ministry of Finance (MoF); the National School for Administration (PNSA); the Palestinian Legislative Council (PLC); the Ministry of Social Development (MoSD); the Ministry of Labour (MoL); the Ministry of Tourism and Archeology (MoTA); the Ministry of Transportation (MoT); the Ministry of Women's Affairs (MoWA), the Ministry of Education (MoE); the Ministry of National Economy (MoNE); the Ministry of Interior (MoI); the Ministry of Agriculture (MoA); the Ministry of Local Government (MoLG); the Attorney General Office (AGO); and the Ministry of Health (MoH).

They thank all employees of these respective institutions that participated in the interviews and data collection process, notably Mahmoud Attaya, Muyad Taleb Suwaiti, Nida Salameh (PMO); Rami Husseini, Shatha Qarshouly, Saja Terawi and Rumoz Jumhour (GS); Kholoud Faroun, Mai Mustapha and Nadi Shawareh (OoP); Maysa Naim and Mohammed Hijazi (GPC); Suad Abu Mashayekh, Areej Asfour, Lina Shalaldeh and Samah Naser (MoJ); Reem Abu Alrub, Samah Sawalhah and Haya Musleh (Diwan); Imran Salahat and Fidaa Musa Abu Hmeid (MoF); Wafaa Hamayel (PLC); Khouloud Abdel Khalik (MoSD); Samer Salameh and Buthaina Salem (MoL); Amin Al-Khatib (MoTA); Farouk Abdel Rahim (MoT); Hanna Nakhleh (MoWA); Mohamad Matar and Assem Qadous (MoE); Bashaer Rabah and Iyad Jaber Assi (MoNE); Ghadeer Abu ElRub and Samah Shaker Joudeh (MoA); Eyad Matakh (MoI); Uhod Enayeh and Islam Zeidan (MoLG); Anas Oury and Nithan Ramadan (MoH); Mustafa Khawaja (Palestinian Central Bureau of Statistics - PCBS).

They would also like to extend their gratitude to other public institutions who participated in the various capacity-building activities organised as part of the project, which also helped inform the Review, notably the Palestinian Anti-Corruption Commission (PACC); the Administrative and Financial Control Bureau; the Energy Authority; and the Monetary Authority.

A number of peers from OECD and other MENA countries participated in the fact-finding missions and capacity-building activities, providing invaluable insights that were integral to the present analysis. The authors wish to warmly thank:

- Ms. Anna Skrjabina, Project Leader, Court Administration of Latvia
- Mr. Manuel Cabugueira, Coordinator of the Technical Unit for Legislative Impact Assessment and Senior Consultant, Portuguese Centre for Planning, Policy and Foresight in Public Administration
- Mr. Ricardo Matias, Program and Project Manager in Portugal's National Press
- Mr. Charfeddine Ghazala, Director General, Office of the Legal Advisor to the Tunisian Government
- Mr. Gianluca Forlani, Judge, Permanent Representation of Italy to the European Union
- Mr. Pétur Berg Matthíasson, Deputy Director, Department of Policy Coordination, Iceland's Prime Minister's Office
- Dr. Rab'ah AL-Ajarmeh, former Minister of State in charge of Public Administration Development, Jordan
- Dr. Francesco Sarpi, Head of Unit for Rationalisation and Improvement of Regulation, Presidency of the Council of Ministers, Italy
- Mr. Peter Kováč, Senior Counsellor, Secretariat of RIA Commission, Ministry of Economy, Slovakia
- Dr. Heba Shahein, Director of Egyptian Regulatory Reform and Development Activity (ERRADA), Egypt

They would also like to thank the European Union for its financial support to the "Support the Palestinian Authority to enhance Governance and the Rule of Law" project, which made this Review possible, and the Office of the European Union Representative (West Bank and Gaza Strip, UNRWA), notably Gerhard Krause, Head of Cooperation, Joris Hereen, Head of Section: Support to Civil Society, East Jerusalem and Governance Issues, and Simona Gallotta, Rule of Law Programme Manager, for their continuous support and their valuable comments. The OECD will develop a complementary Review, as part of the separate "Supporting the Palestinian Authority in Public Administration Reform" project also financed by the European Union, in order to look at other stages of the policy-making process, including policy delivery, monitoring, and evaluation. This project is led by Odoardo Como, Head of Section: Macroeconomic Support, Social Development and Institution Building, and Shereen Abu Eid, Public Administration Reform Programme Manager.

The authors would like to express their gratitude to Xavier Sisternas and Timo Ligi, Senior Policy Advisors within the SIGMA Programme, for their comments.

Finally, they wish to thank the representatives of private sector, civil society and academia who have been active in supporting the project's fact-finding missions and capacity-building activities. These include: Amal Faqih and Omar Rahhal (Human Rights and Democracy Media Center - Shams); Khadijeh Zahran (The Independent Commission of Human Rights - ICHR); Rwa' Jaber and Faten Bolivia (Paltrade); Haitham Zoubi (Exchange Market); Hassan Qustantini (Bethlehem University); Abdallah Hammad (Jerusalem Center for Legal Aid); Majed Aruri (ISTEQLAL); and Mohammed Khader (Birzeit University)

Table of contents

Tables

Figures

Boxes

Abbreviations and acronyms

CBA	Cost-benefit analysis
CEA	Cost-effectiveness analysis
CoM	Council of Ministers
Diwan	Advisory and Legislation Bureau
EU	European Union
GALA	General Administration for Legal Affairs
GS	General Secretariat of the Council of Ministers
HNC	Higher National Committee on the Legislative Plan
MCLP	Ministerial Committee on Legislative Policy
MENA	Middle East and North Africa
MoF	Ministry of Finance
MoJ	Ministry of Justice
OECD	Organisation for Economic Co-operation and Development
OoP	Office of the President
PA	The Palestinian Authority
PCBS	Palestinian Central Bureau of Statistics
PESTLE (analysis)	Political, Economic, Social, Technological, Legal and Environmental
PLC	Palestinian Legislative Council
PMO	Prime Minister's Office
RCA	Root cause analysis
RIA	Regulatory Impact Assessment
ROB	Regulatory Oversight Bodies
SCM	Standard Cost Model

Executive summary

The Palestinian Authority (PA) has been facing several important challenges, from humanitarian emergencies, political stalemates, fiscal deficits and high wage bills to specific governance challenges relating to ministries' weakened capacities for planning or the absence of institutional mechanisms to aptly co-ordinate legislative and policy planning. These challenges have contributed to the Authority's longstanding difficulty in providing adequate public services, in engaging people in the decision-making process and, as a result, in promoting their trust in public institutions. According to a recent survey administered by the Arab Barometer, only 33% of Palestinians reported trusting their public institutions (compared to 51% on average in OECD Member countries).

Rule of law is an important determinant of trust. No other policy area has a greater impact on trust given that rule of law is an essential prerequisite for ensuring the provision of public goods and services, economic development, maintaining peace and order, and the effective control of corruption.

This Review assesses the policy- and law-making processes in the PA, asserting that developing effective policies and legislation is vital to promoting rule of law, better economic and societal outcomes and hence public trust. A policy is a course of action designed to meet a goal or objective, respond to an issue or problem identified by the government as requiring action or reform. Legislation on the other hand are binding laws and regulations, which are typically created by the legislative (laws) and the executive (regulations) branch of government and which can be enforced by a court or government agency. Although separate tools, policies and legislation are interrelated and need to be used in tandem to achieve government objectives.

The Review provides actionable recommendations as well as concrete examples and guidance on how to implement them based on OECD standards and good practices as well as SIGMA standards. The forthcoming *Good Practices Manual for Policy and Regulatory Planning* will also support policy-makers in the PA in the implementation of this Review's recommendations.

Towards improved institutional coordination, problem identification and policy formulation in the Palestinian Authority

The OECD Policy Framework on Sound Public Governance and the SIGMA Principles of Public Administration highlight that institutional coordination, problem identification and policy formulation processes are critical for achieving responsive and efficient governance and service delivery.

When it comes to effective institutional co-ordination around policy formulation the PA faces a number of challenges: the absence of an overall legislative plan to guide the legislative process; line ministries' limited knowledge about legal proposals in progress; unclear mandates and no systematic criteria guiding quality control and financial assessment of new legislation. Problem identification and assessment are hampered by a lack of data and insufficient or ineffective consultation with external stakeholders. Policy formulation and legislative drafting processes do not systematically follow the Authority's 2018 *Legislative Drafting Guidelines* and are instead often based on informal or ad hoc practices.

To improve institutional co-ordination, problem identification and policy formulation, the Palestinian Authority could consider:

- **Streamlining the legislative planning process** to foster more co-ordinated policy- and law-making and facilitate the exchange of draft policies and legislation;
- **Reforming the quality control performed by the centre of government** to reduce functional overlaps and duplication of work and provide policy-makers with more legal expertise and support, notably in the area of legislative drafting;
- **Improving the availability and use of data and evidence for problem identification and assessment,** to ensure accurate understanding of policy issues at an early stage;
- **Promoting inter-ministerial exchanges and liaison with relevant external stakeholders at the early stage of problem identification,** to ensure new legislation account for the pressing policy problems and challenges identified by individual institutions and civil society;
- **Supporting the quality of policy formulation practices,** for example by introducing a designated memo template with guidance and instructions and a new checklist with minimum quality standards for policy proposals.

Regulatory Policy in the Palestinian Authority

The OECD Recommendation on Regulatory Policy and Governance [OECD/LEGAL/0390] highlights that "regulations are one of the key levers by which governments act to promote economic prosperity, enhance welfare and pursue the public interest". When carried out effectively, regulatory policy complements the formulation and implementation of all other policies.

The PA faces issues relating to overlapping mandates for regulatory policy, the administration of ex ante regulatory impact assessments and legislative drafting standards. Regulatory oversight functions are shared by several institutions leading to insufficient quality control of regulatory management tools. Regulatory impact assessments are yet to be carried out in practice, despite an existing formal requirement. The Authority's *2018 Guidelines on Public Consultations* are also found to be inconsistently applied – with non-governmental actors given little opportunity to provide input on draft legislation. Finally, although the PA is committed to updating its body of law to ensure consistency with international obligations, it still lacks a formal requirement to carry out *ex post* evaluations of regulations.

To improve regulatory policy, the Palestinian Authority could consider:

- **Developing and publishing an explicit, formal, and binding whole-of-government strategy for regulatory policy** to clearly allocate leadership responsibilities and operational duties as well as support the operationalisation of strategic objectives;
- **Centralising regulatory oversight functions into one oversight body** to help ensure the implementation of good regulatory practices by providing quality control;
- **Formalising, organising and making systematic the process of forward planning and developing new regulations,** with clear roles and responsibilities of actors involved, to increase transparency and foster buy-in with the changes occurring in the system of better regulation;
- **Introducing ex ante regulatory impact assessment gradually as a default condition for any regulatory proposal** to ensure that regulations meet the needs of businesses and the people;
- **Providing guidance on data collection as part of the legislative drafting guidelines and making use of stakeholder input** to facilitate the use of reliable and relevant evidence in support of the regulatory process;
- **Making the consultation of the public a general requirement for all regulatory interventions,** to ensure that regulations are designed and implemented transparently and in the public interest;

- **Developing a methodology and guidance for ex post evaluation of existing legislation** to ensure that they remain fit for purpose;
- **Carrying out a comprehensive review of the stock of regulations and engaging with stakeholders** to identify the most burdensome areas of existing legislation and ensure that regulations remain up to date, cost effective and deliver the intended policy objectives.

Part I: Towards Improved Problem Identification and Policy Formulation in the Palestinian Authority

1 Overview

This section provides a brief overview of problem identification and policy formulation as critical processes for responsive and efficient governance and service delivery and presents the different thematic sections of Part I.

The OECD is supporting the Palestinian Authority (PA) to enhance governance and the rule of law. The project, funded by the European Commission, aims to contribute to achieving a more effective, transparent and participatory policy- and law-making process set in a clear normative framework, and thus enhance the Palestinian people's and businesses' trust in their public institutions' action. The project includes a review with tailored recommendations that identify opportunities and key areas for improvement on policy- and law-making in the PA.

The policy- and law-making process takes place in a difficult political setting for the PA. Following the 2006 election and the political division between Fatah and Hamas, the activities of the Palestinian Legislative Council (PLC) – the PA's Legislature – were suspended, before the PLC was officially dissolved in 2018. In the absence of a legislature, the President issues decrees. Moreover, humanitarian urgencies as well as an unstable budget situation both on the income and expenditure side represent significant obstacles to legislative planning.

Problem identification and policy formulation are critical processes for achieving responsive and efficient governance and service delivery. Both steps are crucial for sound policy-making. Effective policy development, as highlighted in the OECD Policy Framework on Sound Public Governance (OECD, 2020[1]) is critical to ensuring that governments can translate long, medium and short-term policy goals into concrete courses of action. It also provides an opportunity for governments to collaborate with a broad array of stakeholders and as such is core to the democratic process. It ensures the public governance values - for instance of integrity, openness and transparency, inclusiveness and accountability to name but a few - are adopted widely across government, mainstreamed and integrated not only in the design, but also in the policy implementation process. Translating high-level priorities and the government vision into achievable policies constitutes one of the greatest challenges in policy-making.

Based on the OECD Policy Framework on Sound Public Governance (OECD, 2020[1]) and the SIGMA Principles of Public Administration (OECD/SIGMA, 2017[2]), Part I focuses on the early stages of policy-making with a focus on legislative aspects. It provides concrete and actionable recommendations to the Palestinian Authority to strengthen the problem identification and policy formulation processes of policy- and legislative-making. First, Part I assesses the Palestinian Authority's institutional co-ordination for policy formulation, before it proceeds with analysing different elements of the problem identification and assessment as well as the policy formulation process.

As part of the complementary Public Administration Reform project with the Palestinian Authority, the OECD will develop a complementary review to look at other stages of the policy-making process, including policy delivery, monitoring, and evaluation. This forthcoming review will also assess the role of policy planning units. Part I, therefore, only focuses on the early stages of the policy cycle, namely problem identification and assessment as well as policy formulation.

References

OECD (2020), *Policy Framework on Sound Public Governance*, https://www.oecd.org/governance/policy-framework-on-sound-public-governance/ (accessed on 21 July 2020). [1]

OECD/SIGMA (2017), *The Principles of Public Administration.* [2]

2 Institutional Co-ordination

This section examines institutional co-ordination for improved policy formulation in the Palestinian Authority. It provides an overview of the current institutional framework underpinning the legislative process, highlights the importance of legislative planning for co-ordinated policy formulation and assesses the work of institutions performing the quality control of new legislation.

Low levels of co-ordination limit the PA's ability to identify clear policy priorities, address multidimensional challenges and achieve its strategic objectives. Line ministries only have limited knowledge about the PA's whole-of-government policy agenda. Existing sector or institution-specific strategies are often developed without prior co-ordination with other ministries and consequently lack alignment and take-up. The varying quality of draft legislation renders the work of institutions performing the quality control indispensable, but despite the existence of various quality checks, the roles and responsibilities of the different institutions involved in legal verification and the overall quality control are not sufficiently clearly defined. This section therefore recommends that the PA enhances legislative planning notably by establishing a permanent inter-ministerial planning committee and developing and adopting an annual legislative plan to further streamline the legislative planning process and foster more co-ordinated policy- and law-making. It also recommends to enhance capacity building for policy formulation and legal drafting and to render quality control more efficient notably by reforming the quality control performed by the centre of government, improving the quality of cost assessments and defining and implementing minimum standards for all legislative proposals.

The current institutional framework

Following its founding in 1994, the Palestinian Authority has created an institutional framework and mechanisms based on the rule of law which were enshrined in the Basic Law in 2002 (Palestinian National Authority, 2005[3]). While the Basic Law only contains a "very limited and inadequate" number of provisions that detail the policy- and law-making process (EUPOL COPPS, 2017[4]), it offers an overview of the various institutions involved in the process, ranging from line ministries to institutions providing advisory services, quality control and oversight to decision-making authorities. Apart from the Basic Law, no normative framework exists that regulates the functioning of the PA (EUPOL COPPS, 2017[4]).

According to the Basic Law, the **Palestinian Legislative Council (PLC)** represents the Palestinian Authority's legislature (see Art. 47) (Palestinian National Authority, 2005[3]). It holds the right to legislate and keep the Executive in check. Pursuant to Art. 56 of the Basic Law, the PLC's members also have the right to initiate legislation (Palestinian National Authority, 2005[3]). Besides the PLC, the Council of Ministers (CoM) is the only other institution mandated to initiate legislation. The Internal Regulation on the Palestinian Legislative Council (2000) regulates the review and adoption of draft legislation. Due to the dissolution of the Palestinian Legislative Council in 2007, the current legislative and policy formulation processes of the Palestinian Authority take place in a challenging political context and therefore differ from the one originally established in the Basic Law (see Figure 2.1).

Pursuant to Art. 71.4 of the Basic Law, **line ministries** shall "prepare drafts and legislation related to the ministry and propose them to the Council of Ministers" (Palestinian National Authority, 2005[3]). This article establishes the ministries' responsibility for policy development and legal drafting of draft acts following the initiation of legislation. The Basic Law further stipulates that Ministers are in charge of supervising the conduct of affairs in their respective ministry and are expected to issue the necessary instructions (Art. 71.2) (Palestinian National Authority, 2005[3]). The Basic Law does not contain any additional provisions regarding the different steps line ministries should follow in their internal policy formulation and drafting process (EUPOL COPPS, 2017[4]). Each ministry has a dedicated legal unit that provides legal support and advice, while policy-planning units in line ministries are responsible for co-ordinating and developing policies.

Before draft legislation is submitted to the Council of Ministers, it passes the **Advisory and Legislation Bureau** (Diwan al-Fatwa wa-'Tashri' – hereafter "Diwan"). Created in 1995 by presidential decree, the Diwan reviews all draft legislation (i.e. proposals for laws, bylaws, decrees and decisions) regarding their legislative wording, compliance with the Basic Law and consistency with other existing legislation prior to ratification and publication in the official Gazette.[1] With a body of 12 legal advisers, the Diwan prepares a revised draft of all legislation submitted by line ministries, trying not to alter the nature of the proposed acts. All comments and recommendations made by the Diwan are non-binding. In addition to the legal review, the Diwan provides general legal advice to the PA, including for the adoption and ratification of international agreements. The Diwan is also in charge of publishing the Palestinian Official Gazette.

Following the problem identification and policy formulation phase and after comments from the Diwan are considered by the respective lead ministry, the legislative proposal and an accompanying policy paper on its objective (referred to as policy memoranda) are sent to the **General Secretariat of the Council of Ministers (GS).** The Secretariat verifies all draft acts' consistency with existing legislation prior to submission to the CoM for approval. By virtue of Art. 70 of the Basic Law, the CoM holds the "right to submit draft laws to the Legislative Council, to issue regulations, and to take necessary actions to enforce laws" (Palestinian National Authority, 2005[3]). The Council of Ministers therefore represents a central institution in the PA's institutional architecture. It has decision-making power on all draft legislation that is expected to be submitted to the PLC for discussion and adoption (OECD, 2011[5]). The General Secretariat of the CoM may also create special committees for the review of individual legislative proposals and their corresponding policy memoranda prior to approval by the CoM. Committees may accept, reject or amend legal proposals. By bringing together different relevant ministries and the Diwan, these committees can represent an important forum for intra-institutional co-ordination across administrative boundaries in the absence of the PLC (OECD, 2011[5]).

According to Art. 68 of the Basic Law, the **Prime Minister** not only appoints and removes the members of the Council of Ministers and organises its weekly meetings, but also oversees and co-ordinates the work of the ministers and public institutions. The **Prime Minister's Office (PMO)** was established in 2003, but is not defined by the Basic Law. It provides technical support on an *ad hoc* basis during the policy formulation phase.

According to the regular legislative procedure enshrined in Art. 43 of the Basic Law, the **President** enacts the legislation (Palestinian National Authority, 2005[3]). In case of objections to a legal proposal, the draft law can be returned to the PLC within 30 days. Any objection requires a detailed justification and leads to a new adoption procedure in the PLC (OECD, 2011[5]). The PLC then seeks the opinion of its Legal Committee on the President's amendments or proposal and puts the proposal to a vote. Should a two-thirds majority of the PLC vote in favour of the proposed or original legislation for a second time, the law is considered adopted and must be published in the Palestinian Official Gazette, which exists since 1995. Due to the right to issue decrees, the head of state is considered an ordinary legislative body.

Figure 2.1. The Palestinian Authority's current legislative process

Note: The figure depicts the adjusted legislative process due to the PLC's absence. In the absence of the PLC, there is a gap between the official mandates of the institutions as per the Basic Law and the practice.
Source: Author's own elaboration based on responses received during the OECD's fact-finding mission.

Legislative planning

Multiple factors influence the identification of policy issues and their incorporation into the governance agenda, including the capacity of representative institutions (for instance the centre of government[2]) to co-ordinate on and articulate policy issues. In addition to identifying policy problems and defining challenges that require policy action, policy prioritisation forms an important part of the early stages of policy development process (OECD, 2020[1]). Governments usually do not have resources and capacity to address all problems (simultaneously, at least). They therefore need to prioritise and sequence between various policy projects in the early stages of policy- and law-making to work towards more realistic commitments and better designed government interventions (OECD, 2020[1]).

Strategic planning is a key tool to allow for the co-ordination between different institutions to enhance the quality of policy design and law-making and positively shape policy outcomes (OECD, 2020[1]). Well-embedded legislative planning can be instrumental in translating political commitments and priorities into both long/medium-term strategies and operational action plans that directly guide the work of government. Planning should be systematic, ensuring alignment between various plans as well as between long-, medium- and short-term policy priorities towards a common goal. Strategic planning needs to ensure that policy instruments such as budgeting, regulations and workforce planning are oriented towards this strategy (OECD, 2020[1]).

Across the OECD, the formulation of government policies and legislation is generally based on a planned and co-ordinated process that involves discussions and exchanges between different line ministries as well as actors outside of government. Ideally, all policies and legislation form part of an integrated whole-of-government work programme that may take the form of a strategy or action plan. An example of such an integrated whole-of-government work programme is the Korean New Deal (see Box 2.1).

For strategic planning purposes, the Palestinian Authority has adopted various relevant planning documents. In addition to the multi-year strategic document of the "National Development Plan 2021-2023", different sector strategies as well as cluster operational plans exist. These strategies and plans aim at setting the PA's objectives and priorities and bringing together otherwise scattered policies.

Box 2.1. Integrated whole-of-government work programme in Korea

In the face of the COVID-19 pandemic, Korea adopted the Korean New Deal. This strategic work programme offers a clear vision for a future-proof trajectory. The Korean New Deal builds on a clear and broad vision to transform the country from a fast-follower to a first mover economy, from a carbon-dependent to a low-carbon economy, and from a socially-divided to an inclusive society. These integrated policy priorities are translated in two focus areas: a Digital New Deal and a Green New Deal. This is then further operationalised in key projects. From these projects, ten have been selected as the building blocks of the forthcoming whole-of-government transformation due to their significant contribution to the creation of jobs and new industries, and to a well-balanced form of regional development.

Note: The strategic work programme can be consulted here:
https://english.moef.go.kr/pc/selectTbPressCenterDtl.do?boardCd=N0001&seq=4948
Source: (Government of Korea, 2020[6])

However, despite the existence of a multitude of strategic plans, interviews with various institutional stakeholders revealed that line ministries only have limited knowledge about the PA's whole-of-government policy agenda and the legal proposals in progress. Rather than providing a wider framework for the PA's action, many of the existing strategies and legislative plans are only sector or institution-specific and lack take-up across the whole-of-government. Interviewees further pointed to frequent unexpectedly emerging legal needs and the subsequent development and adoption of legislation that does not form part of existing strategic documents. Due to the associated time pressure and limited resources, these urgent responses may not always meet the quality standards for legal drafting, stakeholder consultation and policy coherence. The OECD's interviews during the fact-finding missions have further shown that limited formal co-ordination mechanisms represent a major challenge for legislative planning. It was reported that in many cases, single pieces of legislation that are not linked to the PA's wider strategies or policy are developed by individual institutions without prior co-ordination with other ministries. This confirms the conclusions from previous reports that "individual institutions producing drafts on their own and pushing them through [...] has become wide-spread practice" (EUPOL COPPS, 2017[4]). Such low levels of co-ordination limit the PA's ability to identify clear policy priorities, address multidimensional challenges and achieve its strategic objectives.

The PA's centre of government (CoG) uses various instruments to ensure greater levels of horizontal policy co-ordination with line ministries and agencies. Responses to the OECD questionnaire show that besides the meetings of the Council of Ministers, inter-ministerial committees at minister, vice-minister and director level (e.g. the Harmonisation Committee led by the Ministry of Justice) also serve as instruments for co-ordination. However, it seems that the PA makes only a limited and inconsistent use of this type of committee (EUPOL COPPS, 2017[4]). The PA confirmed the existence and frequent use of ad hoc working groups that deal with policy issues for a fixed period of time and are composed of representatives of different public institutions (both of line ministries and other institutions or civil society organisations). One example of such temporary working groups are the various special committees that are established by decision of the Council of Ministers to review individual legislative proposals. Contrary to many OECD countries, the PA has not issued any written guidance such as strategic plans, written rules, manuals or guidelines on procedures that may be conducive to co-ordination.

In addition to *ad hoc* co-ordination mechanisms, a standing mechanism exists in theory for the sharing of draft legislation among line ministries prior to the meetings of the cabinet. The General Secretariat of the CoM is required to provide all line ministries with all relevant documentation to enable the provision of comments on draft legislation discussed by the CoM. There is currently no standing mechanism for sharing draft policies among ministries for internal consultation. The PA should consider to further streamline the planning process to foster more co-ordinated policy- and law-making. To overcome the number of challenges related to the fragmentation of the current planning system, the PA should consider reforming the dedicated institutional structures for legislative planning. The PA could foster co-ordination between line ministries on the one hand and line ministries and key units in the centre of government on the other hand by establishing a standing body, such as an inter-ministerial committee to discuss and articulate policy challenges and agree on prioritisation, policies and legislative planning. Such a committee under the chairmanship of the Ministry of Justice could not only help to identify policy conflicts early on, but also help improve visibility of the PA's policy objectives and provide guidance to policy-makers for the preparation of new legislation.

In the past, the PA already had two institutional mechanisms to institutionalise legislative planning. In 2007, the CoM created the **Higher National Committee on the Legislative Plan (HNC)**, which was composed of representatives of line ministries, civil society and the private sector (OECD, 2011[5]), to prepare and implement the PA's annual legislative plan. In 2012, the PA established the **Ministerial Committee on Legislative Policies (MCLP)**, which consisted of the General Secretariat of the Council of Ministers, relevant line ministries and representatives of ministerial committees. Led by the Ministry of Justice, the committee was in charge of presenting legislative priorities and reviewing draft legislation prior to submission to the CoM. It ensured the compliance of line ministry proposals with the "National Sector Plan", the PA's programme and individual ministerial plans, and returned them to the HNC in case of mismatches.

Both the HNC and the MCLP existed for a couple of years, but were eventually discontinued. Despite their dissolution, many stakeholders underscored the beneficial impact of both institutions in terms of co-ordination and planning during the OECD's fact-finding missions. While their functions were to a certain extent overlapping, the PA could consider re-establishing a committee similar to the MCLP that takes on the HNC's responsibilities for the annual legislative plan that sets out the PA's legislative priorities. Without undermining the mandate of the CoM, the committee could be led by the General Secretariat of the Council of Ministers or the Ministry of Justice and consist of a number of relevant ministers and the head of the Diwan. It could build on the reported successful functioning of the Harmonisation Committee under the Ministry of Justice that helps to better co-ordinate the legislative process by analysing the compatibility of all new legislation with the PA's international commitments. Such a committee could be mandated to review draft legislation and the PA's priorities to enhance co-ordination and coherence between the financial, legal and policy planning and legislative drafting between line ministries and the centre of government. Supported by the strategic planning teams in line ministries, it could also help determine the financial costs of legislative projects.

Complementary to a new or strengthened committee, the processes for formulating and drafting individual pieces of legislation should be planned in advance. One way to do this is through the creation of a plan of legislative tasks that is established on a yearly basis through a whole-of-government effort and which is followed by all line ministries for the creation of new legislation. The legislative plan could thus serve as an annual work plan listing specific actions and legislative interventions that are expected to implement the PA's strategic priorities (EUPOL COPPS, 2017[4]). The plan could enshrine the different challenges and gaps in legislation the PA intends to address and provide an overview of the associated priorities. Ideally, the annual legislative plan would specifically list these actions and interventions for all line ministries and include detailed timelines to operationalise them. Each year, line ministries could prepare their sector specific legislative plans (e.g. in specialised sectoral sub-committees) and submit them to the new inter-ministerial committee. The PA could also consider introducing incentives for institutions following the legislative plan and adhering to the included deadlines. An annual legislative plan could thus contribute to further streamlining the legislative planning process.

While the PA first had a legislative plan in 2007, the practice is currently reported to be put on hold. The 2007 version of the plan included the following eight priorities (EUPOL COPPS, 2017[4]):

- Fill in legislation vacuum
- Amend or repeal Israeli military orders
- Amend outdated legislation
- Law packages
- Secondary legislation
- Cost-effective legislation
- Implement international treaties
- Order of amendments

There is currently no overview of the various draft laws and proposals that are being prepared by different entities in the PA. In addition to publishing work plans and legislative plans of line ministries to enhance transparency of the policy development process, keeping a regularly updated overview of individual proposals and their timelines can thus improve legislative planning and help identify bottlenecks and capacity gaps. The current establishment of an electronic file management system under the General Secretariat of the Council of Ministers could be helpful in that regard and help the centre of government track all legislative interventions.

Quality control

Interviewees during the OECD's fact-finding missions pointed to the varying quality of draft legislation across different line ministries. Under the PA's current arrangements, policy formulation and legal drafting fall within the responsibility of the line ministries. While all ministries employ legal staff in dedicated legal units and despite the binding nature (pursuant to Resolution No. 17/174/07 of 2017) of the 2018 Legislative Drafting Guidelines (Palestinian Authority Ministry of Justice, 2018[7]), stakeholders pointed to significant challenges with the quality of legislation. In addition to the overall quality of draft legislation, important parts of the legislative proposals such as impact or background assessments are regularly reported to be missing (for more information see Chapter 8).

The varying quality of draft legislation renders the work of institutions performing the quality check all the more indispensable. In the Palestinian Authority, various bodies are involved in independently ensuring the quality and legality of new legislation. The Diwan reviews referred legislation to verify proposals' legislative wording, compliance with the Basic Law and consistency with other existing legislation prior to ratification and publication in the Official Gazette. A unit in the General Secretariat of the Council of Ministers also engages in quality control to ensure that proposals fit their intended purpose and do not conflict with the Basic Law, before they are sent to the Council of Ministers. A third institution performing quality control is the President's Office, where legal advisors perform a final scrutiny of all draft legislation. The Ministry of Justice also reviews draft legislation from a formal legal perspective, verifies the adherence to legal drafting standards and assesses all proposals' consistency with international treaties.

Despite the existence of various quality checks, the roles and responsibilities of the different institutions involved in quality control are not sufficiently clear, both regarding the legal verification (e.g. legal drafting quality, consistency with existing legislation, compliance with the Basic Law), but also in terms of overall quality control (e.g. alignment with the PA's objectives, affordability, compliance with procedures). This lack of clearly defined mandates leads to overlaps between the functions of different institutions and is reported to have led to misunderstandings and tensions in the past. Close co-ordination may help resolve duplications of work, but currently no formal mechanism exists. In order to improve the efficiency of the quality control on both legal and overall quality of draft legislation and avoid duplication of functions, the Palestinian Authority could consider consolidating the responsibility for legal review and task an institution with the lead on quality control. Due to its expertise, the Diwan could assume this core function. Following the practice in many OECD countries, the Diwan could become a centralised body tasked with providing legal services to public entities (OECD forthcoming, n.d.[8]). Following the current review of its mandate, the Diwan could provide legal information and advice on all draft policies and legislation to the Office of the Prime Minister and the Office of President. It could co-ordinate legal positions with the General Secretariat of the Council of Ministers and line ministries and review the legal conformity of proposals submitted to the Council of Ministers. Moreover, the Diwan could play a more prominent role in capacity building. A strengthened role of the Diwan and more active involvement in the policy- and law-making process will also entail the need for additional staff and budget – a challenge identified by interviewees during the fact-finding mission.

In order to improve the quality of legislative proposals, the PA could consider reforming the quality check by involving the Diwan early on in the policy- and law-making process. While the current system only allows the Diwan to provide comments on final drafts of policies and legislation, a closer cooperation with line ministries *ex ante* could support policy-makers with more legal expertise and support, notably in the area of legislative drafting. Through such an early involvement, the compliance with already existing legislation and the Basic Law could be ensured throughout the process. The Legal Unit in the Office of the President could continue to perform a final legal quality check before legislation is adopted and published.

The Diwan could further expand its already existing legal training programme to give specialised training on policy formulation and legislative drafting to the legal units in the line ministries. In this regard, the allocation of staff members with specialised skills in legislative drafting in all line ministry units could further be conducive to the quality of legislation. Additional exchange of expertise between legal staff in all line ministries, but also in the centre of government's different institutions could also contribute to capacity building. Regular meetings for legal staff can provide a forum to discuss and exchange views on legal drafting across the PA. The PA could thus consider to re-introduce the inter-ministerial workshops on legal drafting that were last held in 2013. A rotation of legal staff in line ministries' legal units with a temporary work placement in the Diwan may further help build capacity for policy formulation.

Another major challenge highlighted during the fact-finding missions, related to the varying quality of costing assessments. While all line ministries are asked to provide an estimation of policy proposals' costs, this assessment is reported to be often of insufficient quality. The PA may thus not only wish to establish procedures to verify that adequate costing was carried out, but also support ministries with their costing assessments. The Ministry of Finance, which verifies the assessment for the Council of Ministers, could help ministries improve their costing assessments. Instead of involving the Ministry of Finance at the end of the policy- and law-making process, its experts could already be invited during the policy formulation phase and participate in the meetings of the policy formulation committees in line ministries to provide assistance with costing assessments. In addition, the Ministry of Finance may consider creating concrete guidance on costing assessments and organising capacity building for line ministry staff.

Beyond the guidance included in the Legislative Drafting Manual, the PA could define and implement minimum standards for the quality of proposals. Similar to checklists for regulatory decision-making (see Part II) (Palestinian Authority Ministry of Justice, 2018[7]), a checklist or dashboard for all policy and legal proposals could further contribute to improving the quality of policy formulation. A checklist could reflect basic information about the proposals, including an overview of the timeline, stakeholder consultation, the Diwan's review, preliminary costing as well as the impact assessment. This tool may also help prioritise and set the agenda for the Council of Ministries. Proposals that do not meet the quality requirements can systematically be identified for remediation. The General Secretariat of the Council of Ministers and the Diwan could help with the preparation and implementation of the checklist. In Finland, for example, the

Bureau of Legislative Inspection in the Law Drafting Department of the Ministry of Justice uses legal drafting guidelines to monitor the quality of all legal proposals (Box 2.2).

Box 2.2. Finland's checklist for policy and legal proposals

In Finland, the government adopted instructions for legal proposals upon presentation by the Ministry of Justice. These instructions lay down common principles and standards. The Government stresses the importance of observing these instructions, so that the Parliament receives the information it needs on the legislative proposals it is to consider. The Bureau of Legislative Inspection in the Law Drafting Department of the Ministry of Justice monitors compliance of the drafting instructions.

The general drafting principles cover:

- A justification regarding the necessity of legislation;
- Legislation must be brief, concise, and clear;
- The factual basis of the proposal must be correct;
- Impact and alternatives must be properly assessed;
- Constitutional issues must be settled;
- The proposed legislation must meet necessary legal, technical and linguistic standards.

The instructions also propose a uniform structure, which must be followed as closely as possible, and the various elements of legislation that must be covered to ensure sufficiently high and uniform quality of all legislation.

Note: The drafting instructions can be consulted here:
https://julkaisut.valtioneuvosto.fi/bitstream/handle/10024/75937/omju_2006_3_bill_drafting_instructions.pdf?sequence=1&isAllowed=y
Source: (Government of Finland, 2006[9])

Recommendations

Recommendation 2.1 - Further streamline the legislative planning process to foster more co-ordinated policy- and law-making.

- Consider reforming the dedicated institutional structures for policy and legislative planning by establishing a permanent inter-ministerial planning committee to discuss and articulate policy challenges, agree on prioritisation, policies and legislative planning. The PA may consider re-establishing the inter-ministerial committee on legislative policies (MCLP). The PMO and the Ministry of Justice may take a leading role in this reform.
- Create an online information and document sharing portal to facilitate the exchange of draft policies and legislation prior to meetings of the Council of Ministers.

Recommendation 2.2 - Develop and adopt an annual legislative plan for the Council of Ministers, containing the priority initiatives, the responsible institutions, deadlines, outputs and outcomes.

- Prepare mandatory annual work plans in line ministries to monitor specific actions and legislative interventions that are planned to implement the PA's strategic priorities.
- Include detailed timelines for individual institutions to operationalise the annual legislative plan.

Recommendation 2.3 - Consider reforming the quality control performed by the centre of government.

- Clearly define the roles and responsibilities of the different institutions involved in quality control regarding the legal verification and the overall quality control in formal mandates to reduce functional overlaps and duplication of work.
- Strengthen the role of the Diwan to create a single institution responsible for providing a quality check of all draft legislation submitted to the Council of Ministers that also provides legal information and advice to the CoG, co-ordinates legal positions with other centre of government units and line ministries.
- Involve the Diwan early on in the policy- and law-making process and establish closer cooperation between the Diwan and the line ministries to provide policy-makers with more legal expertise and support, notably in the area of legislative drafting.
- Consider providing the Diwan with additional staff and financial resources in light of its strengthened role for quality control.
- Expand the Diwan's training programme to provide specialised training on policy formulation and legislative drafting to the legal units in the line ministries.

Recommendation 2.4 - Enhance capacity building for policy formulation and legal drafting.

- Consider introducing, in line with existing capacity, a rotation scheme of legal staff in line ministries' legal units with a temporary work placement in the Diwan to further build capacity for policy formulation and legal drafting.
- Assess existing legislative drafting capacities in line ministries and allocate staff members with specialised skills in legislative drafting in all line ministry units to enhance the quality of legislation.
- Consider creating a policy profession role with functional focal points in each ministry, to strengthen mainstreaming of policy development skills, standards and guidance tools across ministries.
- Establish regular meetings between legal staff in all line ministries, but also in the centre of government's different institutions to provide a forum for discussion and exchange views on legal drafting across the PA. The Prime Minister's Office could call on these regular meetings, while the Ministry of Justice and the Diwan could facilitate the discussions and exchanges to cross-fertilise good practices.

Recommendation 2.5 - Improve the quality of cost assessments for all legislative and policy proposals.

- Establish procedures such as quality checks to verify that adequate costing was carried out for all proposals submitted to the Council of Ministers for approval. The General Secretariat of the Council of Ministers together with the Ministry of Finance could take a lead role for the establishing of these procedures.
- Support ministries with their costing assessments by fostering cooperation with the Ministry of Finance already at the policy formulation phase. The Ministry of Finance could help line ministries improve their cost assessments by involving its representatives in the meetings of the line ministry policy formulation committees. In addition, the Ministry of Finance may consider creating guidance on costing assessments and organising capacity building for line ministry staff.
- Provide line ministries with the Ministry of Finance's expert guidance through a designated manual or guidelines on how to conduct costing assessments of draft legislation, through advisory services

('help desk' approach) or though participation in relevant sessions of the budget committees in line ministries.

- Provide designated training programmes on cost assessments to increase the quality of legislative and policy proposals.

Recommendation 2.6 - Define and implement minimum standards for the quality of proposals

- Consider introducing a checklist or dashboard with basic information about the legislative and policy proposals, including an overview of the timeline, stakeholder consultation, the Diwan's review, preliminary costing as well as the impact assessment for all policy and legal proposals to further contribute to improving the quality of policy formulation. This checklist or dashboard should be aligned with the regulatory process (see Part II). The General Secretariat of the Council of Ministers and the Diwan could help with the preparation and implementation of the checklist.

References

EU Co-ordinating Office for Palestinian Police Support (ed.) (2017), *The Legislative Process in the Palestinian Authority - An Assessment.* [2]

Government of Finland, M. (2006), *Bill Drafting Instructions.* [8]

Government of Korea (2020), *Korean New Deal.* [5]

OECD (2020), *Policy Framework on Sound Public Governance*, https://www.oecd.org/governance/policy-framework-on-sound-public-governance/ (accessed on 21 July 2020). [4]

OECD (2018), *Centre Stage 2 -The organisation and functions of the centre of government in OECD countries.* [9]

OECD (2011), *Regulatory Consultation in the Palestinian Authority - A Practitioners' Guide For Engaging Stakeholders in Democratic Deliberation.* [3]

OECD forthcoming (n.d.), *Review and support of Portugal's State Legal Competency Centre (JurisAPP).* [7]

Palestinian Authority Ministry of Justice (2018), *The Legislative Drafting Guidelines.* [6]

Palestinian National Authority (2005), *Basic Law of the Palestinian National Authority.* [1]

Notes

[1] A new Presidential Decree published on 24 July 2022 further defines the mandate of the Advisory and Legislation Bureau and its role in the legislative process.

[2] The OECD defines the centre of government (CoG) as the body or group of bodies that provide direct support and advice to heads of government and the council of ministers, or cabinet (OECD, 2018[18]). Following responses to the OECD's questionnaire, the President's Office, the Prime Minister's Office and the General Secretariat of the Council of Ministers are most frequently attributed to the centre of government in the Palestinian Authority.

3 Problem Identification and Assessment

This section reviews the process for problem identification and assessment in the Palestinian Authority, with a particular focus on the systematic use of evidence and the deployment of innovative tools and methods.

The Palestinian Authority uses various forms of data and evidence for problem identification and assessment, but information is not made widely available and is not always up-to-date and comprehensive. There is thus no systematic access to relevant and high-quality data for this stage of policy-making. This section therefore recommends that the PA improves the availability and use of data, promotes more regular use of innovative tools and methods, promotes inter-ministerial exchanges, encourages liaising with relevant external stakeholders, and promotes professional, strategic and innovation civil service skills to support effective problem identification and assessment.

The first step in sound policy-making is properly identifying a problem and designing the right response(s) to address it. Policy-makers need to focus on the observation and analysis of a new issue, challenge or current trend that may require the need to be translated and developed into a policy response. This phase is crucial in the sense that it acts as a filter, by assessing whether a social, economic, political or environmental issue or trend demonstrates the need to be further analysed before a policy is developed or if no action should be taken in this context.

It is thus important that policy-makers fully understand the nature of the challenges that are supposed to be addressed by legislation. The Legislative Drafting Guidelines stress the need for a clear and accurate identification of the policy problem. They recommend the use of digital statistics "to monitor the date of the problem and its development to help us to determine its size and to know if it can develop over time, the relationship of that development to the resulting negatives that could be more severe if there is no attempt or intervention to solve it" (Palestinian Authority Ministry of Justice, 2018[7]). The Guidelines further require policy-makers to clearly differentiate between the actual problem, its outcome and symptoms.

Use of evidence

Responses to the OECD questionnaire show that different types of evidence are routinely used in the problem identification process in the PA. Ministries are reported to systematically review and analyse previous policies every three years to identify new issues that need to be translated into policy. They further use systematic reviews, monitoring and evaluation reports as a basis for problem identification. They further consult public statistics and administrative data, reports from international organisations as well as recommendations of control agencies. Responses to the questionnaire also show that line ministries conduct focus group consultations and interviews in addition to surveys and polls. *Ex ante* and *ex post* regulatory impact assessments as well as horizon scanning and foresight exercises are not used as evidence by any of the surveyed institutions (for more information on regulatory impact assessments, see Part II).

The broad array of different types of evidence used in the problem identification process in the PA's line ministries can positively influence the problem identification process. Questionnaire responses, however, also show that not all information is widely available, up-to-date or comprehensive. This observation is in line with the situation described during the interviews with various PA stakeholders in the OECD's fact-finding missions, where limited access to quality information and data was highlighted as a major challenge.

The Palestinian Authority may thus consider improving the availability and use of data and evidence for problem identification and policy assessment. Data and evidence are crucial to identify policy issues and underpin problem assessment. This relates both to availability of the data, the quality of the data and the processes in place to leverage the data for policy-making. The Palestinian Authority could thus consider mobilising already existing data more systematically. Often line ministries collect data (e.g. from the evaluation of previous policies), but do not fully analyse and use it for problem identification and assessment. In addition, they could leverage accessible data and insights from different non-institutional stakeholders such as the Palestine Area Chamber of Commerce, international organisations or civil society organisations (CSOs). A second recommendation is to develop a systematic approach to the collection and management of data relevant for problem identification and an understanding of when this data should be available – e.g. annually, quarterly - to inform the problem identification process. Due to the line ministries' responsibilities, such an approach should be developed at ministry level and in cooperation with the Palestinian Central Bureau of Statistics.

Innovative tools and methods

In addition to the availability of good quality evidence, a number of tools and methods (see Box 3.2 for an overview) can help to identify issues that a government should act upon. The PESTLE framework can help structure context analysis, problem-tree analyses can be used to define causalities and prioritise problem dynamics and the design thinking method can be deployed to apply a user-centric approach to problem definition. Responses to the questionnaire, however, showed that the PA's line ministries use a limited number of these tools. For instance, the Diwan and the Ministry of Justice report the use of SWOT analyses as a tool. Moreover, the Diwan makes use of root cause analyses and institutional assessments by external experts. While the current limited use of a number of tools is a good starting point, the PA's line ministries could promote more regular use of these instruments and deploy a wider array of tools and methods for improved problem identification. In addition to Box 3.2, more detailed descriptions and user guidance of PESTLE, problem-tree analysis and design thinking can be found in the forthcoming OECD Good Practices Manual for the Palestinian Authority (OECD, forthcoming).

In addition to the limited guidance on the "planning stage" provided in the binding Guidelines on Legislative Drafting, a number of line ministries have developed additional guidance on the policy development process that also includes more detailed information about the problem identification phase. For instance, the Ministry of Local Governance and the Ministry of Education prepared respective guidelines to assist their ministries' policy-makers. Recognising the risk a proliferation of guidance documents poses, this useful practice of providing additional guidance on the problem identification and assessment, for instance on the use of problem identification instruments, could be further mainstreamed across all line ministries. The Prime Minister's Office and the Ministry of Justice could take the lead to improve overall practice and avoid a fragmentation of guidance across the PA. New Zealand's Policy Project (see Box 3.1) is an example of how guidance is communicated and skills and capability development are facilitated in an OECD Member country.

Box 3.1. Building Policy Development Capacity in New Zealand: The Policy Project

The Policy Project in New Zealand aims at building a high performing policy system that supports and enables good government decision-making and policy development. The Policy Project is a platform that equips policy practitioners with access to relevant instruments and tools, best practices, advice and information to develop their skills and capability for more effective and better government decision-making. The platform includes links to policy improvement frameworks, a policy methods toolbox, case studies, links to policy communities, insights briefings, and development pathways. It provides a dedicated policy community which regularly interacts to provide common standards to support change at a systemic and not only individual level. The long-term insights briefings have been put in place to ensure that the policies go beyond the urgent to tackle longer-term challenges.

The Policy Project is anchored in the Department of the Prime Minister and Cabinet. It is co-developed with policy practitioners from across government and championed by a network across ministries of deputy chief executives with policy responsibilities, who serve as ambassadors of the Policy Project within their institution or agency.

As part of the Policy Project, three improvement frameworks have been co-designed with the policy community to help government agencies improve their policy quality and capability: the Policy Quality Framework, the Policy Skills Framework, and the Policy Capability Framework.

Policy Quality Framework

The Policy Quality Framework provides the policy community with a set of standards that specify what good quality advice means. Government agencies can use the Policy Quality Framework's standards to hold themselves accountable for the quality of their advice, and to support better government decision-making. Policy advisors and managers can use the framework to help them develop quality policy advice and to peer review the advice of others.

Policy Skills Framework

The Policy Skills Framework sets out the knowledge, applied skills and behaviours that policy practitioners require to deliver quality policy advice. The framework recognises different levels of capability - from new professionals developing their policy craft to seasoned experts at the top of their game. If you are a policy practitioner, you can use the framework to help you map your skills. If you are a policy manager, you can use the framework to help you evaluate your team's skills. Tools based on the framework support individual performance development and building high performing policy teams.

Policy Capability Framework

The Policy Capability Framework is an organisational improvement tool. It describes the key components of policy capability needed by a government agency or team to produce quality policy advice. The Framework provides a common language for government agencies to reflect on policy performance and identify areas for improvement, while being flexible enough to apply in different operating contexts. Senior leaders and policy managers use the Framework to improve the policy performance of their teams and agencies.

Note: The Policy Project can be found here: https://dpmc.govt.nz/our-programmes/policy-project
Source: Government of New Zealand, The Policy Project, https://dpmc.govt.nz/our-programmes/policy-project/about-policy-project (Government of New Zealand, n.d.[10])

To foster a co-ordinated approach across the PA and allow for a comprehensive definition of policy problems, inter-ministerial exchanges are important at the early stage of problem identification. Exchanges between line ministries allow policy-makers to receive information about other institutions' legislative intentions prior to the policy formulation and drafting phase. The various *ad hoc* special committees that are established by decision of the Council of Ministers to review individual legislative proposals should thus not only discuss draft legislation, but could also serve as a forum to exchange views on different policy problems and challenges policy-makers identify and wish to respond to. Ministries could thus prepare and exchange draft legislative proposals at an early stage through policy memoranda (and potentially related documents) including a detailed problem definition to inform each other about challenges and issues they identify and their respective legislative intentions. Such practices would allow for a discussion of the definition of policy problems from different line ministry perspectives. Early-stage policy memoranda may further help staff with the drafting of legislation. The General Secretariat of the Council of Ministers could co-ordinate and facilitate this exchange of policy memoranda.

Therefore, it is advisable to make a ministry's work plans, the related timetables and working groups accessible to all other ministries, either through the digital file management system or through the General Secretariat of the Council of Ministers. This enables ministries interested in a particular legislative or non-legislative project to signal their interest in it, with a view to being represented on the working group or being consulted. Of course, the prerequisite is careful maintaining and regular up-dating of material and databases available.

Box 3.2. Tools and methods for problem identification and assessment

PESTL(E): This tool is a framework for the analysis of key factors (political, economic, sociological, technological, legal and environmental) of the external environment of the policy in question. It comprises a checklist of areas to be examined when analysing these factors. It is used to determine the external factors that have or will have an enabling or hindering impact on the policy and which are later either translated into opportunities and threats in the SWOT analysis or used independently.

SWOT analysis: SWOT is one of the most popular tools for analysing the external and internal environment of the policy in question. It is a relatively simple technique that can be used to support the preparation or amendment of policies, and it often follows on from a PESTL analysis. S (strengths) and W (weaknesses) represent internal factors, while O (opportunities) and T (threats) cover external enablers and limitations.

Root cause analysis (RCA): Root cause analysis is a systematic process for identifying the root causes of policy problems. While several different approaches to RCA exist, they generally include the same four steps: 1) identify and describe the problem in detail; 2) create a timeline from the normal situation up to the time the problem occurred; 3) distinguish between the root cause and other causal factors; 4) establish a causal link between the root cause and the problem.

Problem-tree analysis: The "problem tree" technique is a tool, which is useful in the identification and analysis stages. A problem tree usually consists of several levels, a hierarchy of interlinked problems. In this hierarchy, a problem at a lower lever (in conjunction with other problems at that level) leads to the problem positioned one level above it. Connecting lines indicate cause-effect relationships. In the following example, three levels of problems are shown (with the fourth, fifth etc. lower levels continuing downwards).

A more detailed description of these tools and methods for problem identification and definition can be found in the OECD's forthcoming Good Practice manual for the Palestinian Authority.

Source: Author's own elaboration based on the OECD's Good Practice Manual for the Palestinian Authority (forthcoming).

The quality of the problem identification and assessment can further be improved by tapping wider sources of information and perspectives through increased stakeholder engagement already at the early stages of the policy cycle. The OECD Recommendation of the Council on Open Government [OECD/LEGAL/0438] recommends that governments "grant all stakeholders equal and fair opportunities to be informed and consulted and actively engage them in all phases of the policy-cycle and service design and delivery". The participation of people and civil society can help policy-makers obtain the views of the public, identify potential conflict lines, and gather additional information on previously overlooked issues that require the government's attention. While the OECD's 2011 Guide on Regulatory Consultation in the PA (OECD, 2011[5]) points out that the actual consultation should not start too early, as stakeholders need concrete proposals to comment upon, it is equally important to keep stakeholders from across society already informed at the early stages. At an early stage in the decision-making process, there is still scope to influence and shape policy decisions and outcomes. The PA's line ministries should thus liaise with relevant stakeholders in areas they intend to legislate, in order to profit from their information, knowledge and opinions that can help detect new or emerging policy issues. In addition to early-stage *ad hoc* consultations, line ministries may consider setting up sectoral policy dialogues to regularly exchange views with external stakeholders.

As with all steps of the policy process, the quality of draft legislation depends on the knowledge and skills of the civil service. To identify and define policy problems it is important to develop professional, strategic and innovation skills. Civil servants need to be capable of detecting and understanding the root causes of policy challenges. This requires "analytical skills that can synthesise multiple disciplines and/or perspectives into a single narrative" (OECD, 2017[11]) including the capacity to interpret and integrate different and sometimes conflicting visions correctly, and to refocus and reframe policies. This also includes networking and digital skills to identify the right stakeholders and the right experts outside the civil service for engagement in problem identification. To foster the development of skills and capability for problem identification, the Palestinian Authority should thus include problem identification in all public service training courses related to policy development.

Box 3.3. The Legislative Drafting Guidelines on Problem Identification

The existence of a certain problem is considered a main cause for the failure of the existing legislation, provided there is an applicable legislation, and despite its implementation in reality, there is still a problem. However, if we are talking about a problem that is not addressed by any legislation or PA intervention to solve it, it is imperative to identify the problem clearly and accurately. It is preferable if we have digital statistics that monitor the date of the problem and its development to help us to determine its size and to know if it can develop over time, the relationship of that development to the resulting negatives that could be more severe if there is no attempt or intervention to solve it.

When the history of the problem is studied, attention should be paid that there is a difference between the problem, its outcome and its symptoms; for example: the existence of a Traffic Law, with the existence of congestions on some roads. In this respect, it is necessary to determine if the problem is the inability of the applicable legislation to address this issue, or if the party tasked to implement it is not acting as expected from it, or if the members of the community do not abide by the law, or if the problem lies in the narrow roads and the failure to distribute traffic. If we assume that the congestion is the narrow roads, congestion would then be an occasional factor with traffic accidents being the outcome.

The determination of the problem and differentiating it from the symptoms and the outcomes helps the PA to take the proper decision. This is in addition to the determination of those themes accurately without there being any room for interpretation or independent reasoning, with the necessity to clarify the risks that could result from that problem if the situation stays intact. Non-compliance with the standards of accuracy during the preparation of the document leads to a weakness in its contents on the one hand, and on the other hand it would not reflect the PA's real approach to solve the problem. It is necessary to draft the document in clear language understood by policy-makers to evaluate the extent of intervention, its size, and the suitable time for that intervention and what are the actual needs to be provided.

Source: Palestinian Authority, Ministry of Justice (2018), Legislative Drafting Guidelines, (Palestinian Authority Ministry of Justice, 2018[7])

Recommendations

Recommendation 3.1 - Improve the availability and use of data and evidence for problem identification and assessment.

- Mobilise data that already exists in line ministries more systematically for problem identification and assessment.
- Leverage accessible data and insights from different non-institutional stakeholders such as the Palestine Area Chamber of Commerce, international organisations or CSOs.
- Develop a systematic approach to the collection and management of data (e.g. from the evaluation of previous policies) needed for problem identification. Due to the line ministries' responsibilities, such approach should be developed at ministry level and in cooperation with the Palestinian Central Bureau of Statistics. The PA should provide guidance on data collection as part of the legislative drafting guidelines.

Recommendation 3.2 - Promote more regular use of innovative tools and methods for problem identification and assessment.

- Encourage and train ministries to use a wider array of various instruments and methods for improved problem identification, including PESTL(E), SWOT analysis, root cause analysis and problem-tree analysis.
- Mainstream and promote the use of additional uniform guidance on the use of problem identification instruments across the PA. The Prime Minister's Office should co-ordinate the development and promote this additional guidance document with the help of the Ministry of Justice.

Recommendation 3.3 - Promote inter-ministerial exchanges at the early stage of problem identification.

- Foster a co-ordinated approach to policy- and law-making by exchanging different institutions' legislative intentions in the various special committees prior to the policy formulation and drafting phase to ensure a comprehensive definition of policy problems.
- Use the various ad hoc special committees that are established by decision of the Council of Ministers to exchange on different policy problems and challenges individual institutions wish to react to.
- Encourage line ministries to exchange their legislative policy memoranda (and potentially related documents) at an early stage, to inform each other about their legislative intentions. The General Secretariat of the Council of Ministers could co-ordinate and facilitate this exchange.

Recommendation 3.4 - Liaise with relevant external stakeholders to identify and define policy problems

- Ensure that line ministries liaise with relevant stakeholders in areas they intend to legislate, in order to profit from their information, knowledge and opinions that can help detect new or emerging policy issues. Implementation of the consultation guidelines should be supported and enforced by a body outside of the ministry carrying out the consultation. The Diwan may take the lead in providing the oversight function for stakeholder engagement to identify and define policy problems.

- Consider setting up sectoral policy dialogues between line ministries and external stakeholders to regularly exchange views in addition to early-stage ad hoc consultations.

Recommendation 3.5 - Promote professional, strategic and innovation civil service skills to enable staff to detect and identify policy problems.

- The Palestinian Authority should include specific references to problem identification methods in all related public service training courses.

References

Government of New Zealand (n.d.), *The Policy Project*, https://dpmc.govt.nz/our-programmes/policy-project. [2]

OECD (2017), *Skills for a High Performing Civil Service*, OECD Public Governance Reviews, OECD Publishing, Paris, https://doi.org/10.1787/9789264280724-en. [4]

OECD (2011), *Regulatory Consultation in the Palestinian Authority - A Practitioners' Guide For Engaging Stakeholders in Democratic Deliberation*. [3]

Palestinian Authority Ministry of Justice (2018), *The Legislative Drafting Guidelines*. [1]

4 Policy Formulation

This section assesses the processes in place in the Palestinian Authority for the policy formulation stage. It describes and evaluates the use of existing law-drafting guidance and stakeholder engagement practices and focuses on building capacity for sound policy formulation.

The Palestinian Authority's practices for policy formulation vary across line ministries and are often based on informal and ad hoc processes, which leads to an uneven quality of policy proposals and draft legislation. This section therefore recommends that the PA provides adequate technical guidance, capacity building and training to officials through various means to support harmonised and qualitative policy formulation practices across the administration.

The second step in sound policy-making is designing the right response(s) to address a previously defined problem or challenge. In an ideal setting, policy formulation includes the discussion and drafting of policy options to address societal needs and challenges and translate policy vision into actual policy. In theory, policy formulation therefore includes the identification, assessment, discussion and drafting of policy options to address societal needs and challenges (OECD, 2020[1]). An important part of the formulation stage is policy design, where policy-makers plan the implementation, monitoring and evaluation stages. Analysing and weighing the political, economic, social and environmental benefits and costs of different policy actions thus forms the core of the policy formulation phase (OECD, 2020[1]).

Governance capacity failures such as limited financial, human and technological resources, or governance design failures such as the shortcomings of the institutional framework or inadequate regulations are a few of the numerous barriers to policy design that can consequently hamper efficient policy implementation and service delivery (OECD, 2020[1]).

The use of law-drafting guidance

Pursuant to Art. 74, the Palestinian Authority's Basic Law assigns line ministries the responsibility to "prepare drafts and legislation related to the ministry and propose them to the Council of Ministers" (Palestinian National Authority, 2005[3]). Line ministries are thus not only in charge of policy development, but also for drafting legislation. As in many OECD countries' constitutions, the Basic Law does not provide additional detail on the policy formulation and drafting process of laws and does not stipulate requirements for laws and policies. While the drafting process is often dealt with in regular laws or secondary legislation, the PA currently does not have such legislation including provisions on policy formulation and drafting (EUPOL COPPS, 2017[4]). In most line ministries, policy-planning units are directly involved in the development and preparation of draft acts and policies.

To reduce discretion and ensure uniform standards and quality, many countries make use of guidelines and manuals for the law-drafting process. Similar to many countries in the region, the varying quality of legal drafting across the PA prompted it to commission a guidance document. Addressing the need for improved and uniform drafting practices across the different institutions, the Diwan, the Institute of Law at Birzeit University and the Legal Department of the Legislative Council developed the Guidelines on Legislative Drafting and Guidelines on Secondary Legislative Drafting in 2000 (EUPOL COPPS, 2017[4]). The binding nature of the Guidelines has led to their use in many line ministries, however, during the OECD's fact-finding missions, some interlocutors reported the limited take-up of the document and challenges with its user-friendliness. The PA may thus consider to provide additional training on the use of the Guidelines to ensure they are applied consistently across the PA.

Evidence collected through the OECD questionnaire and within the framework of the fact-finding missions with PA representatives, shows that different practices for policy formulation exist across the PA's line ministries. Ministries' policy formulation processes are often based on informal or *ad hoc* practices. These diverging practices result in an uneven quality of policy proposals and draft legislation that are submitted to the CoM for decision. The EU Co-ordinating Office for Palestinian Police Support finds that compared to ministries' legal proposals, drafts developed by special committees created by the CoM often lack a link to existing policies and require further problem identification and assessment (EUPOL COPPS, 2017[4]). The OECD's interviews also showed that legislation was mostly focused on emergency issues rather than aimed at addressing policy issues in the medium or longer-term.

In the absence of formal requirements for the formulation of policy proposals, a number of existing tools can be developed or further enhanced to support the quality of policy formulation practices. The quality of the official memoranda accompanying draft legislation that are sent by line ministries to the Council of Ministries, can be enhanced through a designated memo template with guidance and instructions. By specifying what information (e.g. objectives, rational, regarding stakeholder engagement) needs to be included, the CoM can directly influence the policy formulation process. The General Secretariat of the Council of Ministers can take a leading role in improving the memorandum's format based on the guidance included in the Legislative Drafting Manual (p. 23) (Palestinian Authority Ministry of Justice, 2018[7]). Similar to checklists for regulatory decision-making (OECD, 2011[12]), a new checklist for policy proposals can further contribute to improving quality standards. The checklist may reflect basic information about the proposals, including an overview of the timeline, stakeholder consultation, Diwan review, preliminary costing, impact assessment.

Stakeholder engagement

The policy formulation process provides an opportunity for governments to collaborate with people, business and CSOs, to innovate and deliver improved public service outcomes (OECD, 2020[1]). Stakeholder engagement does not only allow policy-makers to tap into a wider information and knowledge basis, but also helps prevent policy capture (OECD, 2020[1]). The OECD/SIGMA Principles of Public Administration (Principle 11) therefore recommend to put consistent procedures in place across ministries to enable effective public consultation, allowing CSOs and people to participate and influence government policy (OECD/SIGMA, 2017[2]).

The PA's 2018 Guidelines on Public Consultations recognise the importance of stakeholder engagement "throughout the legislation preparation process". The Guidelines stress however that consultation is particularly important during the legislative policy preparation stage, which is considered to be the "most essential stage for consultation, as it sets for general legislative policy for the proposed legislation and it affects its framework" (Palestinian Authority Ministry of Justice, 2018[13]).

Despite the binding nature of the Guidelines on Public Consultations, interviewees reported inconsistent application across the PA's line ministries. The OECD's fact-finding mission further revealed that non-institutional stakeholders have little opportunity to provide input on draft legislation during the policy formulation phase and contribute to the development of legislation. The PA may thus consider to further mainstream guidance on stakeholder consultations. In particular, the Prime Minister's Office and the General Secretariat of the Council of Ministers may play a role in promoting of this guidance document across the PA.

Capacity for sound policy formulation

Translating policy issues into policy responses and legislation is a complex and technical process, requiring not only subject-matter and legal expertise, but also a sound understanding on how policies are implemented and delivered, and how the policy response may affect the wider policy environment. The right skills for policy development are therefore of critical importance for the policy formulation stage. Policy-makers require a set of skills that bring together traditional aptitudes, such as the capacity for providing evidence-based, balanced and objective advice while withstanding political and partisan pressure, with a new set of skills to meet expectations for digital, open and innovative government, technological transformations and the increasing complexity of policy challenges (OECD, 2020[1]). Policy-makers need to know when and how to deploy institutional and administrative tools for policy formulation and design.

There is thus the need to build professional, strategic and innovation skills in order to develop appropriate policy responses to previously identified issues and challenges. Policy-makers should be able to identify and make use of internal and external resources to further improve policy solutions (OECD, 2020[1]). They need to understand what has worked in the recent past, draw lessons from this experience and identify best practices that can be adapted to current problems (OECD, 2020[1]). The OECD's Policy Framework on Sound Public Governance (OECD, 2020[1]) further advises that senior policy-makers involved in policy formulation acquire skills to understand the political environment and identify the right opportunities to move forward with policy initiatives and to advise decision-makers on different options and trade-offs. In addition to technical knowledge, they thus need to be able to consider political and social values issues (OECD, 2020[1]) and recognise and manage risk and uncertainty (OECD, 2020[1]). Lastly, skills to communicate policy ideas (e.g. including visual presentation and storytelling skills) can help facilitate the exchange with higher-level decision-makers (OECD, 2020[1]). The United Kingdom has developed a framework for skills and knowledge for policy professionals (Box 4.1) and in Northern Ireland both training and guidance are provided to policy practitioners (Box 4.2).

Box 4.1. Policy Profession Standards in the United Kingdom

Developed by the UK Policy Profession as part of the Civil Service, the UK Policy Profession Standards describe the skills and knowledge required by policy professionals at all stages of their career and provide the competency framework for their professional development. By codifying the core skills of policy practice, the framework is designed to support the multidisciplinary teams so critical to effective policy-making – bringing together the domain knowledge, system expertise and specialist skills required to solve public policy challenges more effectively for communities and citizens.

The Policy Profession standards framework has 2 parts:

1. a core document outlining the structure of the standards and learning outcomes, providing a summary of the skills, knowledge and activities that make up individual standards;
2. an annex of detailed descriptors setting out the specific skills for each learning outcome, designed for those who are applying the standards in their own organisation and require a deeper understanding to support capability-building or workforce planning.

The Policy Profession Standards serve as a tool for guidance and assessment related to policy development skills and capacity.

Source: Government of the United Kingdom, UK Civil Service, Policy Profession, (Government of the United Kingdom, 2021[14])

Box 4.2. Capacity building for policy formulation in Northern Ireland

In the United Kingdom, think tanks and educational institutions offer various courses and trainings to strengthen the capacities of civil servants in regards to policy formulation. The Northern Ireland government built further onto this with the creation of a practical policy guide tailor-made to fit its own public service and context. The guide provides a starting point to help those working on developing or reviewing policy identify what issues they need to take into account to ensure that policy is evidence-based, focused on outcomes, forward looking, 'joined up', and meets Northern Ireland requirements. It aims to provide tools, skills and advice that help to develop high quality and effective policy. It does so by setting out a number of common and interdependent elements of the policy development processes.

Note: The policy guide can be consulted here: https://www.executiveoffice-ni.gov.uk/sites/default/files/publications/ofmdfm_dev/practical-guide-policy-making-amend-nov-16.PDF
Sources: Government of Northern Ireland (United Kingdom), (Northern Ireland Executive, 2016[15])

During the OECD's fact-finding missions, various institutional interlocutors reported a strong need to improve public officials' skills and capacities in a number of areas. Officials' skill sets for policy formulation are an important factor for improving the quality of legislation. Human resources management should thus continue to be a strategic priority of the PA.

First, a major challenge highlighted during the OECD's interviews were the legal drafting skills of staff at the President's Office, in the Diwan and most importantly in line ministries. While individual good practices exist, interviews held during the OECD's fact-finding missions showed that legal staff do not always have the required competences with regard to legal wording and drafting. The OECD thus identifies a growing need to increase continuous and regular legal drafting training inside the PA to cope with the challenges of producing laws and regulations of improved quality. Even though all ministries' legal units employ staff familiar with the legislative process, staff members with training in legislative drafting do not exist in all institutions. Equipping all public entities engaged in legal drafting with adequately trained personnel should thus be an imperative for the Palestinian Authority.

Second, additional capacity needs within line ministries relate to skills on budgeting/costing assessments of policy proposals. Following the OECD/SIGMA Principles of Public Administration, policy-makers should be able to cost different policy options, to identify the source(s) of funding for the proposed policy, and to verify if the proposed option is linked to financial planning and affordable within current budgetary agreements (OECD/SIGMA, 2017[2]). In case a policy is not affordable, policy-makers require knowledge to provide an explanation of deviations and the need for additional funding (OECD/SIGMA, 2017[2]). Beyond designated training programmes on costing assessments, the Ministry of Finance can provide expert guidance, for example through a designated manual or guidelines, through advisory services ('help desk' approach) or though participation in relevant sessions of the budget committees in line ministries.

Third, developing capacity to conduct *ex ante* impact assessments as part of the policy formulation process could help overcome challenges related to their systematic use reported during the OECD's fact-finding missions. The OECD/SIGMA Principles of Public Administration recommend that clear and transparent methodologies and criteria should be available for analysing the potential impacts of new policies, including for defining issues/problems and objectives, identifying and appraising alternative policy options and analysing their potential impacts (benefits, costs, anticipated effects and risks) (OECD/SIGMA, 2017[2]). While core elements of impact assessment are included in the legislative drafting guidelines (Palestinian Authority Ministry of Justice, 2018[7]), they are rather high-level, abstract and not sufficiently clear and detailed for policy-makers (see Part II). In addition to the lack of practical guidance, there is currently no dedicated training on impact assessment methodologies in the PA.

In order to enhance staff capacity related to policy formulation, the PA could consider various possible points of action. Continuous training opportunities for all staff involved in policy-making are important to enhance capacity. Targeted training on policy formulation, drafting and impact assessment that complements the existing high-level guidance can help increase the quality of policy proposals. Some OECD Member countries have developed specific government training courses focused on policy formulation and legal drafting, while other countries created external training opportunities in partnership with universities and specific legal institutions. The Netherlands has, for instance, established the Academy of Legislation to improve the quality of legal drafting training in government. In Switzerland, the Legal

Department of the Ministry of Justice works together with Swiss universities to offer training courses. Other examples of efforts to train policy-makers involved in drafting also exist in the MENA region. In Tunisia, the El Manar University offers trainings in cooperation with the government. In the case of the PA, a deepened partnership with academia and specialised training institutes can help to expand existing training courses on policy formulation and design. The trainings provided by Birzeit University, a public university in the West Bank, could thus be extended to ensure that all dedicated staff working on policy formulation and drafting have the possibility to participate. Alternatively, targeted training could also be provided by the Ministry of Justice or the Diwan. All training offers should be centralised in one institution to the extent possible, to ensure a concerted approach to capacity-building across all responsible bodies. Ministries should allocate funding in particular to enable entrants to obtain induction training in policy formulation and drafting. While it cannot replace learning on the job, the provision of formal induction training in policy formulation, e.g. through practical exercises, can have added value by providing a basic understanding of policy formulation procedures and techniques, which will help to accelerate skills development. Such induction training have been established in a number of OECD Member countries, but are currently not yet available in the PA.

Many countries continuously innovate drafting procedures and techniques. To avoid a fragmentation and ensure systematic adoption across government, it is therefore important to introduce all policy-makers involved in drafting to new innovations and practices. Previously hired legal drafters should be offered a course to upgrade their skills. International partners may also be able to support these efforts with additional capacity building programmes. The regional cooperation and peer exchange with neighbouring countries may further be conducive to reviewing and enhancing existing guidance and training programmes.

The identification of pockets of good practice in lead institutions could also help to enhance the policy formulation in other entities through staff rotation schemes that enable skilled staff to share their expertise within a hosting institution. This can be organised through individual or temporary arrangements such as staff on loan schemes or through a more systematic approach in the form of a staff rotation programme. Representatives of the PA highlighted that also the high frequency of staff turnover has led to a loss of important skills and knowledge of institutional processes, methods and information. Enabling staff to rotate between different institutions may thus not only positively influence capacities, but also help mitigate the issue of high staff turnover that was highlighted previously by EU COPPS.

As provided for in principle 12 of the OECD Recommendation on Public Service Leadership and Capability [OECD/LEGAL/0445], the PA could adjust the conditions for workforce mobility and adaptability. It should evaluate existing capacity and enable and encourage short- and medium-term assignments of staff in different institutions when current capacity allows. These assignments could foster learning and exchange of information, promote co-ordination between different entities and occasionally meet short-term labour demands. An example of a workforce mobility programme is the White House Leadership Development Program (see Box 4.3), which rotates 15-20 high-performing line ministry officials into the White House to work on cross-cutting issues and provide leadership development training.

Box 4.3. The White House Leadership Development Program (WHLDP)

The White House Leadership Development Program (WHLDP) engages a diverse annual cohort of GS-15 career employees to work on the federal government's highest priority and highest impact challenges. The Program is sponsored by the Executive Office of the President (EOP) and supported by the Performance Improvement Council (PIC).

Develop Talent: Cultivate the next generation of career senior executives through a rotation focused on the complex, cross-agency challenges that increasingly confront the Federal Government while incorporating a development component to build and strengthen enterprise leadership skills. Key Objectives:

- Provide Fellows a broad federal perspective on high-priority challenges.
- Provide Fellows with access to senior decision-makers.
- Develop Fellows as a cadre of leaders with the skillsets and networks to address challenges through a cross-agency lens and implement solutions across organisational boundaries.

Deliver Results: Harness top talent from across the government to support implementation of key priorities and address mission critical challenges, such as Cross-Agency Priority (CAP) Goals. Key Objectives:

- Strengthen on-going implementation efforts on specific Administration initiatives, such as the Cross-Agency Priority (CAP) Goals that require collaboration and co-ordination among multiple organisations.
- Strengthen long-term strategic planning to ensure delivery of tangible results.

Source: https://www.pic.gov/whldp/ (Government of the United States of America, n.d.[16])

In addition to training, technical-level exchanges and meetings across institutions on policy formulation and drafting can help build capacity. Similarly to the above-mentioned meetings for legal staff to discuss legal developments, meetings of staff involved in policy formulation and drafting may serve as a platform for knowledge-sharing and could further help to build interpersonal contacts.

Recommendations

Recommendation 4.1 - Provide additional training on the use of the Guidelines on Legislative Drafting and Consultation.

- Support line ministries with the implementation of the PA’s two mandatory guidelines by providing training to staff.
- Promote and include in whole-of-government communication efforts the use of the Guidelines on Legislative Drafting and Consultation with the help of the Diwan and the Ministry of Justice.

Recommendation 4.2 - Support the quality of policy formulation practices.

- Enhance the quality of the official memoranda accompanying draft legislation that are sent by line ministries to the Council of Ministers, for example through a designated memo template with guidance and instructions. By specifying what information (e.g. objectives, rational, regarding stakeholder engagement) needs to be included, the Council of Ministers can directly strengthen the policy formulation process.

- The General Secretariat of the Council of Ministers can take a leading role in improving the memorandum's template based on the guidance included in the Legislative Drafting Manual.
- Introduce a new checklist for policy proposals to further contribute to improving quality standards. The checklist may reflect basic information about the proposals, including an overview of the timeline, stakeholder consultation, Diwan review, preliminary costing, impact assessment.

Recommendation 4.3 - Equip all public entities engaged in legal drafting with adequately trained staff.

- Provide designated training programmes on 1) impact assessment methodologies and 2) policy formulation and drafting to increase the quality of policy proposals. Introduce all drafters to new practices and innovation related to drafting procedures and techniques to ensure that they will be adopted consistently throughout the public service.
- Ensure adequate resources are available in line ministries to enable new civil servants to obtain induction training. Previously hired legal staff involved in legal drafting should be offered continuous training courses to upgrade their skills.
- Enable technical-level exchanges and meetings of staff involved in policy formulation and drafting across institutions to help build capacity, foster interpersonal contacts and build a community of practice led by the General Secretariat of the Council of Ministers.

Recommendation 4.4 - Establish cooperation with external partners for capacity building.

- Deepen partnerships with academia and specialised training institutes to expand existing training courses on policy formulation and design.
- Extend the training programmes provided in cooperation with Birzeit University to ensure that all dedicated staff working on policy formulation and drafting have the possibility to participate.
- Encourage international partners to support regional cooperation and peer-to-peer exchanges with countries facing similar challenges to review and enhance existing guidance and training programmes.

Recommendation 4.5 - Support workforce mobility where feasible to share good practice for policy formulation and foster learning and exchange of information across different institutions.

- Adjust the conditions for workforce mobility and adaptability where feasible, by enabling and encouraging short- and medium-term assignments of staff in different institutions through presidential decree.
- Introduce individual or temporary arrangements such as staff on loan schemes or through a more systematic approach in the form of a staff rotation programme to foster capacity building.

References

EU Co-ordinating Office for Palestinian Police Support (ed.) (2017), *The Legislative Process in the Palestinian Authority - An Assessment*. [3]

Government of the United Kingdom (2021), *UK Civil Service Policy Profession*. [8]

Government of the United States of America (n.d.), *White House Leadership Development Program*, https://www.pic.gov/whldp/ (accessed on 18 October 2021). [10]

Northern Ireland Executive (2016), *A practical guide to Policy Making in Northern Ireland*. [9]

OECD (2020), *Policy Framework on Sound Public Governance*, https://www.oecd.org/governance/policy-framework-on-sound-public-governance/ (accessed on 21 July 2020). [1]

OECD (2011), *Assessment Report - The Legislative Drafting Manuals of the Palestinian Authority*. [5]

OECD/SIGMA (2017), *The Principles of Public Administration*. [6]

Palestinian Authority Ministry of Justice (2018), *Guidelines on Public Consultations*. [7]

Palestinian Authority Ministry of Justice (2018), *The Legislative Drafting Guidelines*. [4]

Palestinian National Authority (2005), *Basic Law of the Palestinian National Authority*. [2]

Part II: Regulatory Policy in the Palestinian Authority

5 Political Context

This section provides a brief overview of the political and legal context of the Palestinian Authority informing the regulatory policy process.

Since the establishment of the Palestinian Authority in 1994 and its legislature, the Palestine Legislative Council (PLC), there have been significant changes in the structure of its executive. The PA does not have a formal constitution. The Basic Law, which was promulgated by the President in 2002 and subsequently amended in 2003 and 2005, provides an interim constitution for the PA. It sought to establish a multiparty democratic parliamentary system based on the principle of separation of powers, with the people as the source of power and the rule of law as the basis for governance. (EUPOL COPPS, 2017[1])

Regulatory policy in the PA can only be properly viewed within the context of an extremely complicated political and legal environment. The law is a blend of regulations issued under several political regimes, dating as far back as the Ottoman Empire. As in Jordan, the law is a blend of Islamic customary law, *Urf*, and the principles of Islamic *Shari'a* (the main source of legislation), the stock of legislation applied or enacted under the Ottoman Empire (1516-1917), British Mandate Law (1917-1948), Jordanian legislation applied to the West Bank and Egyptian legislation applied to the Gaza Strip (1948-1967). There have also been subsequent Israeli amendments to previous legislation applicable in areas which were introduced by military orders, and, of course, legislation enacted by the Palestinian Authority since 1994. This legacy creates a significant challenge when drafting new legislation. The "fragmentation of the laws" and low public confidence in the judiciary poses strong challenges for implementing and enforcing laws (OECD, 2011[2]).

The President of the PA is directly elected for a four-year renewable term and is supported by an administrative and organisational body, the Office of the President (OoP). The PA has held presidential elections twice. The first were in 1996 and won by Yasser Arafat. Mahmoud Abbas was elected President 2005. The Palestinian Liberation Organisation's Executive Committee extended his mandate in 2009. In January 2021, President Abbas issued a presidential decree setting dates for elections — starting with elections for the PLC; followed by those for the presidency. However, on 29 April 2021, President Abbas indefinitely postponed the electoral process citing Israel's refusal to permit the inclusion of East Jerusalem. In addition, in March 2020, President Abbas issued a presidential decree expanding the administrative and financial powers of his Office.

The PMO was created in 2003 to manage day-to-day activities of the Palestinian Authority and support the OoP with developing policies. Initially, prime ministers were Fatah members, reflecting the party's electoral majority in the PLC. Following Hamas's election in the 2006 legislative elections, Ismail Haniyeh became prime minister and the role of the PMO became more independent and 'technocratic': first under Salam Fayyad (2007-2013); and then under Rami Hamdallah (2013-2019). The latter formed a short-lived coalition endorsed by Hamas in June 2014. In March 2019, President Abbas appointed Mohammad Shtayyeh as prime minister. (European Council on Foreign Relations, 2021[3]).

Since 2007, legislative competences have been assigned to the President due to the absence of a functioning legislature, the PLC. Since the 2006 election and the political division between Fatah and Hamas, the PLC has not been able to govern. The President can rule by decree in cases of necessity that cannot be delayed and when the legislature is not in session, based on Article 43 of the Palestinian Basic Law (see Box 8.2 in chapter 8). Once the PLC resumes its work, the legislature will have to approve all decrees issued by the President during its first meeting.

Furthermore, a different law-making process has operated in the West Bank than in the Gaza Strip since 2007, as a result of the political division between Fatah and Hamas. In the Gaza Strip, the PLC passes legislative enactments in line with the normal legislative process by adjusting PLC internal procedures. For example, to ensure an integrated voting process, the Gaza-based PLC has introduced the use of authorisations obtained from PLC members, who are held in Israeli prisons. The two parties have categorically refused enforcement of the legislative acts issued by the other. (Institute of Law, Birzeit University, 2017[4])

In the absence of a normal law making process, this report and its recommendations are all the more relevant and necessary. These recommendations will assist the PA to put place a comprehensive regulatory policy, establish processes for a transparent rulemaking process and ensure regulatory quality. However, given the unique political context of the PA, there is a clear need to put in place the basic building blocks of effective governance, including establishing a functioning legislature and consolidating the legal systems of the West Bank and Gaza.

References

EUPOL COPPS (2017), *The Legislative Process in the Palestinian Authority*. [1]

European Council on Foreign Relations (2021), *Mapping Palestinian Politics*, https://ecfr.eu/special/mapping_palestinian_politics/presidency/ (accessed on 7 September 2021). [3]

Institute of Law, Birzeit University (2017), *Report on The Legislative Status in the Palestinian Legal System following the Internal Palestinian Political Divide: 2007-2017*, Ramallah, Birzeit, Palestine. [4]

OECD (2011), *Regulatory Consultation in the Palestinian Authority: A Practioners Guide for Engaging Stakeholderes in Democratic Deliberation*, https://www.oecd.org/mena/governance/50402841.pdf. [2]

6 Strategy and Vision for Regulatory Policy

This section describes the extent to which the Palestinian Authority has developed an explicit regulatory policy strategy, linking better regulation initiatives to specific policy goals. It recommends actions to enhance PA's regulatory policy strategy.

The Palestinian Authority has put in place some elements of a regulatory policy in its legislative drafting and consultation guidelines, and some of these elements are being implemented on an ad hoc basis. The benefits of good regulatory practices are not yet communicated systematically. This section therefore recommends that the PA puts in place a whole-of-government strategy for regulatory policy and an overarching communication strategy.

The objective of regulatory policy is to ensure that regulations are made in the public interest. It addresses the permanent need to ensure that regulations and regulatory frameworks are justified, of good quality, and "fit-for-purpose".

Building on that idea, the OECD developed the Recommendation of the Council on Regulatory Policy and Governance [OECD/LEGAL/0390] (see Box 6.1) to advise governments on how to develop an explicit, dynamic, and consistent "whole-of-government" policy to pursue high-quality regulation.

A whole-of-government strategy for regulatory policy serves to express the government's commitment to high-quality regulation and to support the process of translating the PA's strategic directions and objections into interventions aimed at economic growth and people's well-being. At the same time, the strategy helps to formalise and organise the process of regulatory reform by clearly assigning roles and responsibilities of the actors involved in regulation making.

Box 6.1. The 2012 Recommendation of the OECD Council on Regulatory Policy and Governance

The OECD Recommendation on Regulatory Policy and Governance [OECD/LEGAL/0390] provides governments with clear and timely guidance on the principles, mechanisms and institutions required to improve the design, enforcement and review of their regulatory framework to the highest standards; it advises governments on the effective use of regulation to achieve better social, environmental and economic outcomes; and it calls for a "whole-of-government" approach to regulatory reform, with emphasis on the importance of consultation, co-ordination, communication, and co-operation to address the challenges posed by the inter-connectedness of sectors and economies.

The Recommendation advises governments to:

1. Commit at the highest political level to an explicit **whole-of-government policy for regulatory quality.** The policy should have clear objectives and frameworks for implementation to ensure that, if regulation is used, the economic, social and environmental benefits justify the costs, the distributional effects are considered and the net benefits are maximised.
2. Adhere to **principles of open government**, including transparency and participation in the regulatory process to ensure that regulation serves the public interest and is informed by the legitimate needs of those interested in and affected by regulation. This includes providing meaningful opportunities (including online) for the public to contribute to the process of preparing draft regulatory proposals and to the quality of the supporting analysis. Governments should ensure that regulations are comprehensible and clear and that parties can easily understand their rights and obligations.
3. Establish mechanisms and institutions to actively provide **oversight of regulatory policy**, procedures and goals, support and implement regulatory policy, and thereby foster regulatory quality.
4. Integrate **Regulatory Impact Assessment (RIA)** into the early stages of the policy process for the formulation of new regulatory proposals. Clearly identify policy goals, and evaluate if regulation is necessary and how it can be most effective and efficient in achieving those goals.

Consider means other than regulation and identify the trade-offs of the different approaches analysed to identify the best approach.

5. Conduct **systematic programme reviews** of the stock of significant regulation against clearly defined policy goals, including consideration of costs and benefits, to ensure that regulations remain up to date, cost justified, cost effective and consistent, and deliver the intended policy objectives.
6. Regularly publish reports on the **performance of regulatory policy** and reform programmes and the public authorities applying the regulations. Such reports should also include information on how regulatory tools such as RIA, public consultation practices and reviews of existing regulations are functioning in practice.
7. Develop a consistent policy covering the **role and functions of regulatory agencies** in order to provide greater confidence that regulatory decisions are made on an objective, impartial and consistent basis, without conflict of interest, bias or improper influence.
8. Ensure the effectiveness of systems for the **review of the legality and procedural fairness** of regulations and of decisions made by bodies empowered to issue regulatory sanctions. Ensure that citizens and businesses have access to these systems of review at reasonable cost and receive decisions in a timely manner.
9. As appropriate apply **risk assessment,** risk management, and risk communication strategies to the design and implementation of regulations to ensure that regulation is targeted and effective. Regulators should assess how regulations will be given effect and should design responsive implementation and enforcement strategies.
10. Where appropriate promote **regulatory coherence** through co-ordination mechanisms between the supranational, the national and sub-national levels of government. Identify cross-cutting regulatory issues at all levels of government, to promote coherence between regulatory approaches and avoid duplication or conflict of regulations.
11. Foster the development of regulatory management capacity and performance at **sub-national levels** of government.
12. In developing regulatory measures, give consideration to all relevant **international standards** and frameworks for co-operation in the same field and, where appropriate, their likely effects on parties outside the jurisdiction.

Source: (OECD, 2012[5])

Regulatory Policy Strategy

OECD Member countries have taken different approaches to introducing a whole-of-government policy strategy to ensure regulatory quality (see Box 6.2).

Box 6.2. Building whole-of-government programmes for regulatory quality

Countries considering the introduction of a policy for regulatory quality across the whole- of- government face the issue of where and how to start the process of embedding regulatory policy as a core element of good governance. An incremental approach has worked in some settings, such as the Netherlands or Denmark, while other countries like the United Kingdom, Australia or Mexico have used a more comprehensive approach.

In Canada, the first whole-of-government policy was introduced in 1999 with the Government of Canada Regulatory Policy, which was later replaced by the Cabinet Directive on Streamlining Regulations in 2007, Cabinet Directive on Regulatory Management in 2012 and the Cabinet Directive on Regulation in 2018. The latest version of the directive sets out the government's expectations and requirements in the development, management, and review of federal regulations. It outlines four guiding principles for departments and agencies:

1. *Regulations protect and advance the public interest and support good government:* Regulations are justified by a clear rationale in terms of protecting the health, safety, security, social and economic well-being of Canadians, and the environment.
2. *The regulatory process is modern, open, and transparent:* Regulations, and their related activities, are accessible and understandable, and are created, maintained, and reviewed in an open, transparent, and inclusive way that meaningfully engages the public and stakeholders, including Indigenous peoples, early on.
3. *Regulatory decision-making is evidence-based:* Proposals and decisions are based on evidence, robust analysis of costs and benefits, and the assessment of risk, while being open to public scrutiny.
4. *Regulations support a fair and competitive economy*: Regulations should aim to support and promote inclusive economic growth, entrepreneurship, and innovation for the benefit of Canadians and businesses. Opportunities for regulatory co-operation and the development of aligned regulations should be considered and implemented wherever possible.

Source: (Treasury Board of Canada Secretariat, 2018[6]); (OECD, 2010[7])

Such a whole-of-government policy is yet to be introduced in the Palestinian Authority. The 2002 Basic Law, like constitutional legislation, assigns legislative competencies to the Council of Ministers, the Prime Minister and the Ministers, in addition to the President under the extraordinary procedure. It does not however contain any further provisions on how legislation should be prepared, nor on the objectives and frameworks for regulatory policy implementation to ensure beneficial outcomes to the economy and society.

The PA has committed to underpin its regulatory interventions on a number of good regulatory principles in its guidelines on legislative drafting and public consultation, reflecting OECD good practice. Albeit not explicitly, the guidelines prepared by the Ministry of Justice with the support of the OECD, and later that of EUPOL COPPS, serve as the normative basis for better regulation in the Palestinian Authority.

The need for coherent and uniform practices in drafting legislation was identified shortly after the establishment of the PA. In an effort to formalise the legislative drafting process, the *Guidelines on Legislative Drafting* and *Guidelines on Secondary Legislative Drafting* were developed in 2000 and 2004 by the Advisory and Legislation Bureau[1], the Institute of Law at Birzeit University and the Legal Department of the Legislative Council. (EUPOL COPPS, 2017[1]) The OECD conducted an assessment of these guidelines and developed a separate *Practitioners' Guide on Regulatory Consultation*, which helped strengthen the PA's legislative process (see Box 6.3).

Box 6.3. OECD's 2011 *Assessment Report of the Legislative Drafting Manuals* and *Practitioners' Guide on Regulatory Consultation*

From 2009 to 2013, the OECD was engaged in a partnership with the Palestinian Authority (PA), the MENA-OECD Initiative to Support the Palestinian Authority (MIP), to assist in the implementation of core public governance reforms. The partnership was financed by the Government of Norway in a solid institutional platform coordinated by the Ministry of Planning and Administrative Development.

The project provided a platform to make systematic use of peer learning and policy advice instruments provided by the MENA-OECD Governance Programme in order to support effective change and modernisation of the PA's public administration and public sector in general. It was organised around 4 main streams that include (1) an increased participation of officials in the activities of the MENA-OECD Governance Programme to support effective regional policy dialogue, (2) a series of actions to facilitate the full implementation of the principles of the Rule of Law, (3) specific support to the implement the international standards of integrity in the public sectors to fight corruption, and (4) the use of OECD and MENA good practices to develop e-government systems that support a more efficient and effective Palestinian administration.

As part of the first phase of the MIP (2010-2011), the OECD notably developed an *Assessment Report of the Legislative Drafting Manuals of the Palestinian Authority* and a *Practitioners' Guide on Regulatory Consultation in the Palestinian Authority for Engaging Stakeholders in Democratic Deliberation*.

The Assessment Report was addressed to public officials in charge of legal drafting and regulatory policy. It assessed two legislative drafting manuals, prepared in the PA, in the context of international good practice and made recommendations for both revising their content and making them operationally effective.

The first Report provides an assessment of the legislative drafting manuals which were under review in the PA at the time. Based on international good practice examples, the Assessment Report identifies options to improve the existing two manuals, for primary and secondary legislation, to support the development of a combined and improved manual which would:

- promote coherent and consistent legislative drafting techniques across legal departments that adhere to international standards;
- improve the quality of legislation;
- support clear laws for people and businesses.

The assessment analyses the structure of the possible manual, its content and status, and provides a series of recommendations for improvements. It presents methods to enhance the value of the manual and reinforce its successful implementation. It also asks the question of the relevance of Interpretation Acts in the PA's legislation. The Report's recommendations were eventually reflected in a revised version of the guidelines issued in 2013 by the Ministry of Justice, covering both primary and secondary legislation.

The Practitioners' Guide assesses the regulatory consultation process in the PA and presents good practices examples from OECD countries and practical guidelines. The Guide is based on a survey conducted in May 2010 and the workshop on "Regulatory Policy Tools and Institutions in Practice" organised in Ramallah in July 2010. The survey and workshop were addressed to public officials in charge of legal drafting and regulatory policy. The guide provides guidance to public officials of the Palestinian Authority responsible for regulatory policy and facing choices about the most appropriate form of consultation; it addresses when and how to use public consultation, who to involve and how to overcome barriers for a successful consultation process. In 2013, the PA published its official *Guidelines on Public Consultation* building upon this Guide and the OECD's assessment of consultation practices in the PA.

Source: (OECD, 2011[8]) (OECD, 2011[9])

Renewed efforts initiated in 2015, aimed at giving impetus to the legislative process, led to another review of the Guidelines by a working group comprised of institutions with key competencies in the regulatory process (Advisory and Legislation Bureau (Diwan al-Fatwa wa Tashri'), Ministry of Justice (MoJ), Ministry of the Interior (MoI), Council of Ministers (CoM), Office of the President (OoP)).

The CoM issued the Guidelines in October 2017, thus marking an important step forward towards consistent and coherent legislative drafting. (EUPOL COPPS, 2017[1])

In 2018, the working group issued revised versions of the legislative drafting and the consultation guidelines in cooperation with EUPOL COPPS. The revised guidelines reflect the recommendations for improvement resulting from previous reviews and aim to provide a comprehensive guide to legislative drafting and stakeholder engagement to civil servants tasked with developing regulations.

The ambition was only partially achieved: while the guidelines constitute a good normative basis for regulation making in the PA, they remain relatively high-level. A step-by-step guide to civil servants on how to use tools such as cost-benefit analysis is missing. To address this issue, the Good Practices Manual accompanying this review was developed, which offers selected practical ways to enhance planning and regulatory performance.

In addition, implementation of the guidelines in practice so far has been lacking due to a number of reasons, which are further elaborated in the following sections.

Vision for Regulatory Policy

The leadership of the Palestinian Authority is committed to strengthening the use of evidence and transparency when preparing and implementing laws and regulations, albeit not yet explicitly in formal statements.

The PA's "National Policy Agenda 2017-22: Putting Citizens First" outlines the PA's strategic policy objectives for the benefit of the people. Some of the policy priorities in the agenda can be linked to good regulatory principle (Palestinian Authority, 2016[10]).

In Pillar 1, the PA commits to consolidating and modernising its body of law to ensure consistency with international obligations as a policy priority (Pillar 1, National Policy 3).

Pillar 2 deals with institutional reform (National Priorities 4 and 5), in particular with regards to making the PA more people-centred and effective. This should be realised i.e. by developing and implementing an e-government strategy, which focuses on the delivery of online services to people.

In National Policy 9, the PA seeks to strengthen accountability and transparency in the regulatory process, which according to the Policy Agenda could be implemented by putting in place a mechanism for public consultation on draft legislation.

With regards to impact assessment, the Policy Agenda states that going forward, policies should be assessed in terms of their impact on women and girls and the ways in which they advance principles of gender equality (Palestinian Authority, 2016[10]) – a practice that only few OECD countries carry out systematically.

Communicating the benefits of regulatory reform

Despite the initial efforts to introduce good regulatory practices and promote the better regulation agenda, there are few efforts undertaken to systematically communicate benefits and costs of regulatory reform to the public and within the administration. An overarching communication strategy on regulatory reform is not foreseen as part of the legislative drafting and consultation guidelines. The legislative drafting guidelines do not spell out the benefits of using regulatory management tools, while the public consultation guidelines make some reference to the benefits of stakeholder engagement to inform the regulatory process, such as increased trust in government.

As a result, there is still limited appreciation of the benefits associated with using regulatory management tools as a process to facilitate policy integration and proportionate interventions, and legitimising government decision-making, both within the administration and among external stakeholders.

Recommendations

The "National Policy Agenda" contains some references to good regulatory practice, but a whole-of-government strategy for regulatory policy is missing. The leadership of the Palestinian Authority is committed to strengthening the use of evidence and transparency when preparing and implementing legislation. Crucially, the PA outlines plans for strengthening accountability and transparency in the regulatory process in its "National Policy Agenda". A whole-of-government strategy for promoting good regulatory practices across the administration is missing.

The legislative drafting and consultation guidelines are important steps towards strengthening regulatory policy in the PA. The guidelines demonstrate the PA's support for high-quality regulation making. They formalise crucial steps in the regulatory process and mostly follow OECD best practice in this regard. However a more practical, step-by-step guide on how to use different regulatory management tools is missing and implementation in practice is lacking due to a lack of capacities, enforcement and buy-in.

Despite those important efforts to promote better regulation principles, the objectives and results of regulatory reform are not communicated systematically within the administration and to the public. An overarching communication strategy on regulatory reform is not part of the legislative drafting and consultation guidelines and the guidelines themselves do not spell out the objectives and results of regulatory reform. As a result, the benefits of regulatory management tools like RIA are not fully understood across the administration and by external stakeholders, which limits the capacity to gather support and buy-in for reforms across the administration and the general public.

Recommendation 6.1 - Consider developing and publishing an explicit, formal, and binding whole-of-government strategy for regulatory policy. The policy should clearly allocate leadership responsibilities and operational duties throughout the stages of the regulatory process.

- Clearly allocate leadership responsibilities and operational duties throughout the stages of the regulatory process.
- Formulate the whole-of-government strategy in a single high-level public declaration, e.g. a resolution. Such resolution could be prepared by a centre of government body, such as the Prime Minister's Office, to demonstrate the PA's commitment to better regulation principles. All bodies and institutions with key competencies in the regulatory process (PMO, Diwan, GS of the CoM, Ministry of Justice) should be involved in the development of the strategy and roles and responsibilities should be clearly assigned.
- Ensure the strategy includes, as a minimum, the following elements:

- A statement outlining the rationale for the PA to make use of good regulatory principles and how the strategy supports the objectives of the "National Policy Agenda";
- A definition of the core good regulatory principles of – among others – necessity, proportionality, predictability, transparency, simplicity and participation, and the explicit commitment to abide by them when elaborating and adopting new (regulatory) measures;
- A description of the scope and tools of the good regulatory practices to be applied across the PA.

Recommendation 6.2 - Drawing from a whole-of-government strategy, elaborate an Action Plan to organise, schedule, coordinate and monitor the implementation of good regulatory practices.

- Ensure the Action Plan is developed, implemented, and monitored by the centre of government in a joint effort with the Diwan, who is currently developing an Action Plan to support its efforts to better organise the legislative process;
- Include explicit (quantitative) targets, deadlines and performance indicators in the Action Plan. Besides setting the condition for monitoring progress in implementation, such an approach allows to determine whether success is achieved; and ultimately enhances accountability and stimulates refinement and learning. Guidance on how to develop good performance indicators can be found in the Good Practices Manual;
- Feature a comprehensive, sustained and tailored capacity-building programme in the Action Plan to mainstream expertise on the application of good regulatory practices by all relevant divisions;
- Consider including incentive structures such as publishing "naming & praising" reporting mechanisms[2]; and budgetary bonuses and promotions based on objective quality standards and transparent meritocratic criteria to promote compliance with the Action Plan and incentivise ministries to start implementing good regulatory practices.
- Consider consulting external expertise, for example in the form of technical assistance, to support the development and implementation of the Action Plan.
- Incorporate and draw from the practical guidance outlined in the accompanying Good Practices Manual to develop the Action Plan.

Recommendation 6.3 - Consider carrying out efforts to systematically communicate on the regulatory policy strategy and the benefits of good regulatory practices both internally and with external stakeholders to seek progressive buy-in to the principles of evidence-based, transparent decision-making.

- Communicate the benefits of regulatory reform to demonstrate the PA's commitment to high-quality regulation to external stakeholders. It will be crucial to convey the benefits of good regulatory practices for the attractiveness of the business environment. This undertaking should be supported by the centre of government;
- Leverage these efforts to convince businesses and other external stakeholders to deliver missing data and verify existing evidence to inform regulatory impact assessment and, in turn, decision making;
- Convey the purpose, benefits and objectives of good regulatory practices within the administration to generate buy-in in ministries;
- Consider different possible forms and channels for communication including awareness-raising events, targeted trainings on the subject provided to civil servants, and potentially a flyer

advertising the most important benefits of regulatory reform within and outside of the administration.

References

EUPOL COPPS (2017), *The Legislative Process in the Palestinian Authority.* [4]

OECD (2012), *Recommendation of the Council on Regulatory Policy and Governance*, https://legalinstruments.oecd.org/en/instruments/OECD-LEGAL-0390 (accessed on 7 November 2018). [1]

OECD (2011), *Regulatory Consultation in the Palestinian Authority*, https://www.oecd.org/mena/governance/50402841.pdf (accessed on 26 March 2021). [6]

OECD (2011), *The Legislative Drafting Manuals of the Palestinian Authority: Assessemnt Report*, https://www.oecd.org/mena/governance/50402734.pdf. [5]

OECD (2010), *Regulatory Policy and the Road to Sustainable Growth*, https://www.oecd.org/regreform/policyconference/46270065.pdf (accessed on 23 January 2019). [3]

Palestinian Authority (2016), *2017- 22 National Policy Agenda: Putting Citizens First*. [7]

Treasury Board of Canada Secretariat (2018), *Cabinet Directive on Regulation*, https://www.canada.ca/en/treasury-board-secretariat/services/federal-regulatory-management/guidelines-tools/cabinet-directive-regulation.html (accessed on 16 January 2019). [2]

Notes

[1] At the time, the Bureau was part of the Ministry of Justice.

[2] Annual evaluation reports for the implementation of the Action Plan could discuss individual ministries' performance in implementing the Action Plan's measures and praise well-performing ministries.

7 Institutional Framework and Capacities for Regulatory Policy

This section examines the institutional framework for regulatory policy in the Palestinian Authority. Regulatory management needs to find its place in a country's institutional architecture, and capacities for promoting and implementing Better Regulation need to be built up. Mechanisms and institutions need to be established to actively provide oversight of regulatory policy procedures and goals, support and implement regulatory policy and thereby foster regulatory quality.

In the Palestinian Authority, several bodies share regulatory policy functions and competencies for regulatory oversight are spread across different institutions. Overlapping mandates and a lack of co-ordination mechanisms and analytical capacities for regulatory policy hamper effective regulation. Quality control of regulatory management tools is yet to be introduced. This section therefore recommends that the PA formalises inter-institutional co-ordination, centralises regulatory oversight functions in one body, and promotes analytical capacities in line ministries.

The institutional set-up of regulatory policy matters. Regulatory management needs to find its place in a country's institutional architecture and have support from all the relevant institutions. The institutional framework extends well beyond the executive centre of government, although this is the main starting point. The legislature and the judiciary, regulatory agencies and the local levels of administration also play critical roles in the development, implementation and enforcement of policies and regulations.

Key Institutions for Regulatory Policy

In the Palestinian Authority, several bodies share critical regulatory policy functions. Since the establishment of the PA in 1994 and the subsequent coming into operation of its legislature, the Legislative Council, there have been significant changes in the structure of its executive. These developments have led to the creation of a series of bodies related to the drafting process, which have somewhat overlapping functions and changing relationships over time. (OECD, 2011[9])

Office of the President (OoP)

The Office of the President is the administrative and organisational body supporting the President. Its main tasks according to *Law No. (5) 2020 regarding the Palestinian Office of the President* are:

- Organising communication and cooperation with all official and non-official local and international governing institutions and with the private sector;
- Supervising the preparation and implementation of the president's activities on the local level;
- Implementing the president's policies in the social field;
- Following up on the implementation of the decisions and instructions of the President with the competent authorities.

As part of its work, the OoP establishes working groups with public administration and private sector representatives to discuss legal drafts that might concern businesses, civil society, or the general public. The public can also voice concerns with existing legislation directly to the OoP's Complaints Department, which serves as an "open feedback channel".

In March 2020, the administrative and financial powers of the OoP were extended by Presidential Decree. Some legal experts see conflicts of power arise with the PA, as the OoP was granted independent financial authority and the power to work directly with the private sector. (European Council on Foreign Relations, 2021[3])

Prime Minister's Office (PMO)

The Prime Minister's Office (PMO) was created in 2003 to manage day-to-day activities of the PA and support the OoP with developing policies.

The Prime Minister, supported by the PMO, has the following competences according to Art. 68 of the Basic Law:

- Appoint and remove members of the Council of Ministers;
- Organise weekly meetings of the Council of Ministers and setting the meeting agenda;
- Oversee and coordinate the work of the ministers and public institutions;

- Issue necessary decisions within the Prime Minister's competence in accordance with the law;
- Sign and issue regulations approved by the Council of Ministers.

The Basic Law does not clearly define the role and responsibilities of the Office itself.

The "National Group" at the PMO, a body that used to discuss priorities and draft legislation among relevant public entities, reportedly worked effectively but was abolished with the most recent Cabinet change. Its re-establishment could serve to enhance the legislative process.

Council of Ministers

The Council of Ministers has executive and administrative authority in the PA according to Art. 63 of the Basic Law, except for legislation falling under Art.43 (Presidential decrees). Art. 70 of the Basic Law provides that the Council of Ministers shall have the right to transmit draft laws to the Legislative Council, to issue secondary regulations and to take necessary actions to implement laws. This right of course only applies when the Legislative Council is in session and does not apply to legislation falling under Art.43. The CoM also can establish technical committees to look into certain policy issues and to provide the Council with policy recommendations.

General Secretariat (GS) of the Council of Ministers

The General Secretariat provides legal, technical, administrative, and logistical support to the Council of Ministers according to the Cabinet website[1]. The Secretariat also:

- Prepares agendas for Cabinet sessions, drafts minutes and recommendations, and issues and announces public decisions;
- Provides technical, legal, and logistical support to ministerial committees;
- Monitors the implementation of the PA's programme and decisions and submits recommendations for improvement to the Council of Ministers;
- Prepares reports for the Council of Ministers on the performance of ministries and institutions;
- Consults with the public on issues with existing legislation through surveys and opinion polls and provides recommendations to the Council of Ministers;
- Reviews drafts laws presented to the Council of Ministers and controls legal quality;
- Prepares regulation in coordination with relevant authorities.

The GS shares the function of reviewing draft legislation and controlling legal quality with the Diwan, the Ministry of Justice, and the President's Legal Adviser, according to information provided in OECD interviews. The General Secretariat and the Ministry of Justice share the responsibility for organising consultations and the GS is also present at all stakeholder consultation meetings. In both instances, a silo-ed approach prevents the sharing of information and best practices.

Advisory and Legislation Bureau (Diwan al-Fatwa wa Tashri')

The Advisory and Legislation Bureau (Diwan) has played a central role in the legislative process since its establishment in 1995 by presidential decree. *Cabinet Resolution No. (6) 2014* approved Diwan's status as an independent body after it was previously affiliated with the Ministry of Justice. The head of the Bureau was assigned the rank of a minister.

Diwan's main functions concerning the regulatory process include:

- The Bureau's Legislation Department reviews the legal quality of proposed and draft legislation prepared by ministries and adjusts the draft if necessary, a process which is referred to as "final drafting";

- The Bureau's Studies and Research Department carries out legal studies and research to support the work of the Bureau and ministries tasked with developing legislation;
- The Bureau also has technical responsibility for supervising legal advisers within ministries, who are charged at the same time with evaluating and reporting on draft legislation submitted to ministries by the Bureau.

Though not strictly part of its mandate, the Diwan evaluates the rationale of draft laws provided by the ministries and, if provided, the quality of the explanatory memorandum.

In addition, the Bureau is required to respond to all legislative and legal matters referred to it by public agencies, in the following cases:

- Legislative and other legal matters referred to it by the President, the Prime Minister, the Speaker of the Legislative Council, ministers or heads of public departments and bodies;
- Disagreement between ministries, public institutions and institutions in any of the legal issues or regulations related to their tasks and powers, and the difference in their application.

In light of its functions, the Diwan is considered the *de facto* regulatory oversight body for the PA, though such a role has not yet been stipulated *de jure* in law.

To this end, the Diwan is currently developing an article to expand its mandate. The article will, if approved by the Cabinet, introduce a legislative quality unit tasked with scrutinising the quality of regulatory management tools (RIA and stakeholder engagement) and supporting ministries in the process of applying them.

Ministry of Justice (MoJ)

The Ministry of Justice provides legal services and advice within the administration and acts as the link between the executive and the judiciary.

Even though not strictly part of its mandate, the ministry organises stakeholder consultations on draft legislation on ministries' behalf on an ad hoc basis, a task that it shares with the General Secretariat of the Council of Ministers. It then collects the feedback provided by stakeholders, responds to comments received, and shares the results with the Council of Ministers.

The MoJ also reviews legal quality of draft legislation, a responsibility that the Ministry shares with the Diwan, the Office of the President, and the GS of the Council of Ministers, which includes the final reading of draft legislation before it is officially issued by the President, according to a Council of Ministers decision of October 2021. It also leads the *Harmonisation Committee*, a joint committee established by the Council of Ministers in charge of reviewing consistency of draft legislation with international treaties.

Ministry of Finance (MoF)

The Ministry of Finance prepares financial policies and manages the public budget. It reviews the financial impacts of legislative drafts prepared by other ministries on an *ad hoc* basis and provides recommendations to the Council of Ministers.

Legislative Council (PLC)

The Legislative Council is the unicameral legislature of the PA. Its activities were suspended following the 2006 elections and the Hamas-Fatah split.

Art. 47 of the Basic Law grants the Council legislative authority. Its role and functions were established in the *Internal Regulations of the Palestinian Legislative Council* in 2000. According to Art. 110 (4) of the Basic Law, the Legislative Council has the right to review the procedures issued by the President during the absence of the legislature.

Regulatory Oversight

International evidence suggests that countries increasingly set up regulatory oversight bodies (ROBs), responding to the demand for a whole-of-government approach to better design, organise and implement regulatory policy. This holds for both OECD countries and other economies.

Regulatory oversight is a critical aspect of regulatory policy. Without proper oversight, undue political influence or a lack of evidence-based reasoning can undermine the ultimate objectives of policy. Careful, thoughtful analysis of policy and an external check of policy development are required to ensure that governments meet their objectives and provide the greatest benefits at the lowest costs to people. The OECD therefore recommends that countries "*establish mechanisms and institutions to actively provide oversight of regulatory policy procedures and goals, support and implement regulatory policy, and thereby foster regulatory quality.*" (OECD, 2012[5])

ROBs may take on various tasks and responsibilities. As a norm, they do not have the right to formulate policies or draft legal acts. ROBs do not appraise the merit and substance of policy choices made by regulatory agencies, either. Rather, their mandates may range from more systemic functions such as coordination, capacity building and advocacy to also embracing individual quality scrutiny (for instance, of single RIA reports). The OECD has stated five key functions that ROBs should be tasked with (see Box 7.1).

Box 7.1. Main features of regulatory oversight bodies

Principle 3 of the 2012 OECD Recommendation of the Council on Regulatory Policy and Governance calls for countries to "**establish mechanisms and institutions to actively provide oversight of regulatory policy procedures and goals, support and implement regulatory policy and thereby foster regulatory quality**". The Recommendation highlights the importance of "a standing body charged with regulatory oversight (...) established close to the centre of government, to ensure that regulation serves whole-of-government policy" and outlines a wide range of institutional oversight functions and tasks to promote high quality evidence-based decision making and enhance the impact of regulatory policy.

In line with the Recommendation, the 2021 Regulatory Policy Outlook [OECD/LEGAL/0390] identified **five "core" functions** that are essential for effective regulatory oversight to be carried out by one or several bodies close to the centre of government or at arm's length:

Table 7.1. Five Core Functions for Effective Regulatory Oversight

Areas of regulatory oversight	Key functions
Quality control (scrutiny of process)	• Monitor adequate compliance with guidelines / set processes • Review legal quality • Scrutinise impact assessments • Scrutinise the use of regulatory management tools and challenge if deemed unsatisfactory
Identifying areas of policy where regulation can be made more effective (scrutiny of substance)	• Gather opinions from stakeholders on areas in which regulatory costs are excessive and / or regulations fail to achieve its objectives • Reviews of regulations and regulatory stock • Advocate for particular areas of reform
Systematic improvement of regulatory policy (scrutiny of the system)	• Propose changes to improve the regulatory governance framework • Institutional relations, e.g. co-operation with international for a

	• Coordination with other oversight bodies • Monitoring and reporting, including report progress to parliament/government to help track success of implementation of regulatory policy
Co-ordination (coherence of the approach in the administration)	• Promote a whole of government, coordinated approach to regulatory quality • Encourage the smooth adoption of the different aspects of regulatory policy at every stage of the policy cycle • Facilitate and ensure internal co-ordination across ministries / departments in the application of regulatory management tools
Guidance, advice and support (capacity building in the administration)	• Issue guidelines and guidance • Provide assistance and training to regulators/administrations for managing regulatory policy tools (i.e. impacts assessments and stakeholder engagement)

Source: (OECD, 2021[11])

The type of authority accorded to a ROB usually depends on its source, i.e. on the institution that created the ROB and the basis of its establishment. In principle, a ROB is the more authoritative the more directly it reports to the centre of the government or to a strong political office, and if it is established through a statutory instrument such as a law or a secondary government regulation.

The institutional framework for regulatory oversight varies significantly among OECD countries (see Box 7.2). In many cases, responsibilities for regulatory oversight functions are split between different ministries or bodies. This set-up raises the issue of effective co-ordination mechanisms between bodies with shared responsibilities and the merits and challenges of a fragmented institutional landscape for regulatory policy. (OECD, 2018[12])

Box 7.2. Institutional set-up for regulatory oversight in selected OECD countries

In the United States, the Office of Information and Regulatory Affairs (OIRA) carries out all key regulatory oversight functions and is located at the centre of government, in the Executive Office of the President. OIRA scrutinises the quality of significant regulations and RIAs and can return draft regulations to agencies for reconsideration if their quality is deemed inadequate. OIRA also co-ordinates the application of regulatory management tools across government, reports to Congress on their impacts, provides guidance and training on their use and identifies areas where regulation can be made more effective.

In Germany, the National Regulatory Control Council (*Normenkontrollrat*, NKR) is a regulatory oversight body operating at arm's length from government. To guarantee independence, the NKR was established by law. This ensures that any change to the NKR's mandate requires a public debate in Parliament. The NKR reviews the quality of all RIAs, provides advice during all stages of rulemaking, and has responsibilities in administrative simplification and burden reduction. The Better Regulation Unit (BRU) in the Federal Chancellery is the central co-ordinating and monitoring body for the implementation of the Federal Government's programme on better regulation and bureaucracy reduction.

The United Kingdom's Regulatory Policy Committee is an independent regulatory oversight body made up of eight committee members appointed by the Secretary of State for Business, Energy and Industrial Strategy (BEIS). Committee members are not civil servants and are independently appointed, with no affiliation to government. The Committee provides the government with external, independent scrutiny of evidence and analysis supporting new regulatory proposals in RIAs and ex post evaluations of legislation. The Better Regulation Executive (BRE), located within BEIS, is responsible for better regulation policy and is the lead unit in the UK government for promoting and delivering changes to the regulatory policy framework. The Cabinet Office is responsible for the Guide to Making Legislation and providing training and support to government departments making legislation.

Sources: (OECD, 2018[13]), (OECD, 2021[11]).

Institutional set-up for regulatory oversight in the PA

The Palestinian Authority has a fragmented institutional landscape for regulatory policy, and responsibilities for certain regulatory oversight functions are shared by several authorities. There is no formally appointed body responsible for regulatory oversight functions as defined in Box 7.1.

The Diwan, the General Secretariat of the Council of Ministers, the Ministry of Justice, and the Office of the President's legal team share certain oversight functions, like the review of legal quality of draft legislation. There is no formal and systematic mechanism in place to coordinate those functions, which prevents the sharing of information and best practices and hinders an aligned approach.

At the same time, a more in-depth quality control function of regulatory management tools is missing. There is currently no oversight body responsible for asking for or reviewing the quality of regulatory impact assessment, stakeholder engagement, and *ex post* evaluation of legislation. Support and scrutiny by such a body will be a determining factor for an effective implementation of such tools in the PA.

The Diwan seeks to address this gap in the PA regulatory system by establishing itself as the regulatory oversight body, not only *de facto*, but *de jure*. Currently, the Diwan prepares an article expanding its mandate to include the quality control of RIA and ex post evaluation and to make its opinions binding. The new mandate will, among other things, introduce a legislative quality unit tasked with quality control of regulatory management tools and providing support to ministries. The development of the article is currently at a halt.

Co-ordination

The bodies and institutions involved in the regulatory process face significant challenges stemming from a lack of clearly defined co-ordination mechanisms, and a limited and dis-joined identification of roles and responsibilities within institutions and across the PA with regards to the use of regulatory management tools and regulatory oversight.

There is currently no systematic approach in place for sharing draft legislation among ministries for internal consultation. The General Secretariat of the Council of Ministers is formally required to provide the legislative draft to line ministries for comment prior to cabinet review, but implementation in practice is lacking. Despite attempts to institutionalise a coordination mechanism[2], the internal consultation on legislative drafts at the planning and design stage is done on an *ad hoc* basis through the creation of dedicated committees. Upon request, the Council of Ministers can create a special committee to discuss draft legislative proposals among institutional stakeholders directly responsible for the policy area.

More often than not however, ministries do not solicit feedback on their legislative draft. This silo-ed approach to regulation making prevents policy integration and the sharing of best practices between ministries. For example, the law on pathways and streets prepared by the Ministry of Public Works had to be abolished as the Ministry of Transport and the Ministry of Local Governance had not been consulted in the process of developing the legislation.

The limited and disjoined identification of roles and responsibilities in the regulatory process creates additional challenges to the administration. There is an overlap in competencies of bodies with key regulatory competencies and little coordination of their activities.

The Diwan, the Ministry of Justice, the Office of the President's Legal Adviser, and the General Secretariat of the Council of Ministers all share responsibilities with regards to reviewing legal quality of draft legislation. The GS of the CoM and the OoP both provide complaints departments for people, but there is reportedly no effort carried out to coordinate or share the feedback received. The Ministry of Justice and the GS both organise consultations on behalf of ministries and the OoP organises stakeholder workshops with public and private sector representatives. The resulting inefficiencies spill over negatively on the capacity to effectively seek policy integration, build up checks-and balances mechanisms, and leverage existing databases and expertise.

The Council of Ministers has the competence to establish and abolish agencies, units, and other bodies belonging to the executive according to Art. 69 of the Basic Law. This includes the ability to amend the bodies' mandates. Some ministries reported having requested such a change of mandate in the past, to no avail.

This lack of co-ordination and clear competencies poses significant challenges to the administration and may grow with the potential resumption of the Palestinian Legislative Council and the necessary review of all legislation adopted since 2007.

Practical ways to improve inter-institutional co-ordination can include putting in place a permanent forum to discuss draft legislation among ministries (see Box 7.3).

Box 7.3. Inter-ministerial co-ordination in Germany

In Germany, the preparation of bills is mainly the prerogative of the line ministries (*Ressortprinzip*). Before a draft bill is submitted to the Federal Government for adoption, the lead ministry must involve other federal ministries and offices affected by the bill as well as the German body responsible for regulatory oversight, the National Regulatory Control Council, and the Federal Commissioner for Efficiency in Public Administration, at an early stage.

The Chancellery takes on an active role in the inter-ministerial co-ordination during the legislative process. The co-ordinator of the Federal government on Better Regulation (Minister of State to the Chancellor) has to be consulted and gives his/her opinion on each draft according to Section 21 of the joint rules of procedure (GGO). The Better Regulation Unit (BRU) is the responsible working unit, fulfilling this function on behalf of the Minister of State.

The work of the Federal government is based on the principle of consensus: If there are differences of opinion between the main federal ministries involved or between the ministries and the chancellery, "extensive or expensive preparations should not be started or instigated (…)" before the cabinet has agreed on the matter. This also means that ministries will likely address and resolve issues with the quality of the RIA accompanying the legislative draft.

When transmitting the Ministry draft, steps must be taken to ensure that those involved have sufficient time to examine and debate questions falling within their competence. The lead Federal Ministry is responsible for involving all parties, ensuring sufficient time for debate.

Source: (Federal Government of the Republic of Germany, n.d.[14])

Ministerial committees

When there are partnerships or overlaps in the jurisdiction of line ministries, the PA establishes ad-hoc committees to look into certain policy issues and sets their scope of work, mission and the duration of their mandate. These committees present their reports to the Cabinet. For example, the Minister of Social Development has worked with other line ministers on creating ad-hoc committees to ensure effective coordination and avoid overlap, such as the committee to implement the Law on Juvenile Justice, and the committee to review and prepare the Family Protection Bill (FPB).

There is a large number of committees and working groups established to inform the legislative process. This rather resource intensive undertaking does not seem to be carried out in a sufficiently coordinated manner and it is unclear if and how results of such committees are being used to inform the legislative draft.

Co-ordination with the local level

The local councils in the Palestinian Authority play an important role in legislative planning and significantly contribute to the Cabinet's priority setting. These consultations are carried out through workshops that inform the "National Policy Agenda".

The Ministry of Local Affairs is tasked with managing the coordination with the local level of administration. The High Council for Urban Planning and Building prepares the geographical plan that allocates responsibilities for policy implementation per region, and the local councils are tasked with implementation.

Capacities

Overall, the work of the PA is affected by important financial and, most importantly, analytical resource constraints. Capacities for regulatory quality within legal units[3] in line ministries suffer from three main challenges.

First, central institutions and line ministries are often understaffed and legal units responsible for legislative drafting are mostly made up of lawyers and legal specialists. There is a lack of policy analysts with different backgrounds, including economists, social scientists and experts in specific areas of public policy. Where experts and skilled officials are available in pockets of the administration, they often are not allocated the tasks most suitable for their skills and training due to the silo-ed approach to regulation making discussed above. Hiring and correctly allocating those specialists will be essential for a successful implementation of regulatory impact assessment in practice, for example for carrying out cost-benefit analysis including the assessment of wider social and economic impacts and analysing underlying policy issues.

Second, while best practice guidelines exist, a more hands-on, practical guidance is lacking. The legislative drafting and consultation guidelines represent a significant effort to introducing good regulatory practices in the PA and broadly reflect OECD best practice. Core elements of both regulatory impact assessment and stakeholder consultation are mentioned in the guidelines, but are yet to be implemented in practice. This is partly due to the lack of concrete, hands-on guidance explaining in detail how different tools like cost-benefit analysis and stakeholder engagement techniques can be carried out in practice. The existing guidelines remain high-level and touch upon good regulatory practices in an abstract manner, leaving room for interpretation. Civil servants not familiar with those practices will need more detailed instructions for them to be able to implement RIA and stakeholder engagement in practice. The Good Practices Manual accompanying this review offers selected practical guidance in this regard.

Third, there is a limited offer of targeted training on policy development and legal drafting, and training on RIA and engagement techniques is missing. Trainings on legislative drafting have been delivered by Birzeit University, but they have not led to the development of uniform practices across the PA. There are also trainings offered by the Ministry of Justice and the Diwan on legal drafting and – quality that target legal departments in line ministries. However, these trainings do not live up to the needs of the administration and have not achieved the desired results. There are no targeted trainings available on regulatory impact assessment and public consultation, though the consultation guidelines stipulate the Ministry of Justice provide training on the latter. The lack of practical guidance that complements the rather high level guidelines exacerbates the need for targeted trainings, particularly on RIA, stakeholder engagement, and the *ex post* evaluation of existing legislation.

Recommendations

Within the PA, the competencies for supporting regulatory quality are distributed among several key ministries and institutions. As is the case in some OECD countries, the PA has a fragmented institutional landscape for regulatory policy, and several authorities share responsibilities such as organising consultations or ensuring legal quality. A lack of clear roles and procedures and the dis-joined allocation of mandates leads to an overlap of powers and un-coordinated action between institutional actors, which in turn affects the PA's capacity to effectively seek policy integration and establish a system of checks and balances.

In practice, a lack of co-ordination and a silo-ed approach to policy and regulation making still hinders effective regulation making. Structural inter-institutional dialogue on assessments of policy issues, evidence-based rule making and co-ordinated regulatory responses are not fully systematised in the PA. Timing and duration of such exchanges are not explicitly set. Furthermore, no clear mechanism is in place in case differences emerge between public bodies in terms of priorities and agendas or of the evidential basis they brought forward. The lack of co-ordination also prevents ministries and other bodies from sharing best practices, information, and data.

There is no body responsible for the promotion of the better regulation agenda and strong leadership from centre of government is missing. Political support from the centre of government pushing for regulatory reform is crucial for high-quality regulatory management. First steps to demonstrate such support have been taken with the adoption of the legislative drafting and consultation guidelines. Still, there is a need for a body with the power to enact change across the administration to promote the better regulation agenda. This need is amplified by the co-ordination issues in the legislative process and the lack of implementation of the good regulatory practices outlined in the guidelines.

The PA operates under significant analytical capacity constraints. There is a lack of financial and human resources and need for capacity-building to support the use of impact analysis and other good regulatory practices. Some efforts to build analytical capacities in the form of trainings have been launched by Birzeit University, the Diwan, and the Ministry of Justice, but so far have had limited effect. Training and capacity building for the use of RIA and other regulatory management tools is missing. In addition, legal departments in ministries consist mostly of lawyers that lack the experience needed to carry out analyses of financial, economic, social, and environmental impacts of regulations.

Regulatory oversight functions are shared by several institutions and quality control of regulatory management tools is missing. Certain oversight functions, like the review of legal quality, are shared between the Diwan, the Ministry of Justice, the Office of the President's Legal Adviser, and the General Secretariat of the Council of Ministers. Crucially, there is no single body formally responsible for carrying out quality control of regulatory management tools. Introducing such function will be essential to the successful implementation of regulatory impact assessment, stakeholder engagement, and *ex post* evaluation of existing regulation in the PA. The Diwan is currently developing an article aiming to include such function in its mandate, but implementation is stalled.

Recommendation 7.1 - Consider putting in place designated leadership driving a concerted better regulation effort across the administration.

- Designate a body with the authority to enact change across the administration and to promote a co-ordinated whole-of-government approach to regulatory policy. To this end, this body should be tasked with overseeing the implementation of the whole-of-government strategy and Action Plan in Recommendation 6.1. and 6.2.
- Consider placing these functions in the centre of government, where the body will have the authority necessary to promote and co-ordinate better regulation reform efforts across the administration. In this respect, the PMO could be considered to play an important role.

Recommendation 7.2 - Foster inter-institutional coordination to enhance co-operation and complementarity between line ministries, the Diwan, and key relevant units in the Presidency and the Prime Minister's Office.

- Formalise an institutional co-ordination mechanism to achieve effective policy integration and regulation making. This mechanism should take the shape of a standing body, such as a ministerial committee under the chairmanship of the Ministry of Justice, as suggested in *Law No. 4 1995*.
- Consider alternatively to re-establish the "National Group" at the PMO (or create a similar structure) and task it with the sharing and discussing of draft legislation and public priorities among ministries. The group would be well-positioned at the centre of government for promoting co-ordination within the administration.

Recommendation 7.3 - Consider centralising regulatory oversight functions into one oversight body, so that they are explicitly and permanently embedded in the regulatory process. This body should also be tasked with ensuring the implementation of good regulatory practices by providing quality control.

- Consider creating a single regulatory oversight body entrusted with a clearly defined mandate, powers and resources. The Advisory and Legislation Bureau (Diwan) would be well positioned for taking on the role as a single regulatory oversight body. Its independent position and respected authority makes the Bureau the ideal body to carry out an oversight function. In addition, the Diwan has recently been allocated additional human resources, effectively better positioning it to take on new functions. The efforts currently under way to expand the Diwan's mandate will help establish the Bureau as a *de jure* ROB and should be pursued.
- In terms of the mandate of the ROB, consider the following tasks:
    - contributing to the elaboration of the Regulatory Policy Action Plan, referred to in Recommendation 6.2. above;
    - coordinating the overall regulatory policy implementation;
    - providing guidance to ministries on the application of good regulatory practices such as forward planning, RIA, consultation and *ex post* evaluation, complementing the existing guidelines;
    - upon request by ministries, advising and assisting on procedural and methodological aspects related to good regulatory practices;
    - carrying out a procedural review, i.e. ensuring that the thematic divisions comply with the RIA, consultation, and evaluation requirements, and a substantive review, i.e. that the good regulatory practices meet agreed minimum quality standards such as soundness and robustness of the evidence presented;

  - issuing opinions to the attention of the ministries on the extent to which they meet due process standards and regulatory quality standards;
  - reporting regularly on the status of regulatory policy in the PA, providing statistical information on the progress rate and the quality of implementation. The reporting activity should include the identification of common problems encountered by ministries as well as recommendations for further improvements of the system; and
  - contributing to the design, organisation and delivery of initiatives to build regulatory policy capacity within the PA.
  - By definition, the ROB should not be involved in the elaboration of policy choices with should remain in the hands of the ministries.
- In terms of the powers of the ROB, allow for a transition period while regulatory management tools are gradually implemented in practice. The ROB's opinions would be progressively enforced to allow for sufficient time for ministries to develop good regulatory practices with the ROB's support;
- Ensure that the General Secretariat of the CoM provide support to the new ROB by conducting a first formal review of the documents submitted, i.e. confirming all necessary elements have been submitted and potentially screening out problematic or particularly burdensome RIA statements for the ROB's review;
- Allocate an adequate number of expert staff with appropriate professional background, including (but not exclusively) in law and economics to support the ROB in carryout its functions.

Recommendation 7.4. – Strengthen analytical capacities within the administration to conduct effective and efficient regulatory impact assessment, stakeholder engagement, and ex post evaluation.

- Make civil servants systematically aware of and trained in using regulatory management tools (RIA, stakeholder engagement, *ex post* evaluation). All civil servants responsible for drafting or reviewing regulations should know of their obligations and duties. They should also be trained in various techniques to carry out impact assessment and evaluation and gather input from stakeholders;
- Make senior civil servants cognitive of the effects of regulatory management tools on the quality of regulations and regulatory framework. This can be achieved i.a. with the systematic communication of the benefits of regulatory reform within the administration as proposed in Recommendation 2.3;
- Provide targeted training on regulatory policy principles, tools and techniques to be conducted possibly by the Ministry of Justice, the Diwan, or Birzeit University. Such training offers should be centralised in one institution to the extent possible, to ensure a concerted approach to capacity-building efforts;
- Complement trainings with practical, step-by-step guidance on how to use the different *ex ante* and *ex post* assessment and stakeholder engagement tools. This will require further developing the existing guidelines for legislative drafting and consultation;
- Invest in expert human resources with different backgrounds (incl. economics and social sciences) both in ministries and the ROB in order to ensure the successful implementation of good regulatory practices.

References

European Council on Foreign Relations (2021), *Mapping Palestinian Politics*, https://ecfr.eu/special/mapping_palestinian_politics/presidency/ (accessed on 7 September 2021). [2]

Federal Government of the Republic of Germany (n.d.), *Gemeinsame Geschäftsordnung der Bundesministerien*, http://www.verwaltung-innovativ.de (accessed on 20 March 2019). [7]

OECD (2021), *OECD Regulatory Policy Outlook 2021*, OECD Publishing, Paris, https://doi.org/10.1787/38b0fdb1-en. [4]

OECD (2018), *Case Studies of RegWatchEurope Regulatory Oversight bodies and the European Union Regulatory Scrutiny Board*, https://www.oecd.org/gov/regulatory-policy/Oversight-bodies-web.pdf (accessed on 3 October 2019). [6]

OECD (2018), *OECD Regulatory Policy Outlook 2018*, OECD Publishing, Paris, https://doi.org/10.1787/9789264303072-en. [5]

OECD (2012), *Recommendation of the Council on Regulatory Policy and Governance*, https://legalinstruments.oecd.org/en/instruments/OECD-LEGAL-0390 (accessed on 7 November 2018). [3]

OECD (2011), *Regulatory Consultation in the Palestinian Authority*, https://www.oecd.org/mena/governance/50402841.pdf (accessed on 26 March 2021). [1]

Notes

[1] http://www.palestinecabinet.gov.ps/portal/Government/GeneralSecretariatEn.

[2] In the past, there had been attempts to establish an inter-institutional consultation process when the draft legislation was submitted to General Secretariat of the Council of Ministers, which was coordinated by the General Administration for Legal Affairs (GALA) of the OoP. Similarly, the *National Group* used to be responsible for coordinating better regulation efforts and reviewing draft legislation at the PMO, and the Ministerial Committee on Legislative Policies was established in 2012 to review draft legislation and discuss policy priorities under the auspices of the Ministry of Justice. Albeit successful, both mechanisms were abolished.

[3] This section discusses the capacities within legal units responsible for legislative drafting. Policy units in charge of policy formulation and design are discussed in Part I.

8 The Development of New Regulations

This section reviews the processes for developing new regulations in the Palestinian Authority, with a particular focus on forward planning, administrative procedures and ex ante impact assessment.

The legislative process in the Palestinian Authority takes place against a backdrop of a multi-faceted political and legal context. The guidelines for legislative drafting reflect international best practice, but practical implementation needs reinforcement. The absence of the Legislative Council amplifies the need for a systematic assessment of regulatory impacts ex ante. This section therefore recommends that the PA gradually introduce RIA in practice and support its implementation by putting in place effective regulatory oversight.

Laws and regulations should be always based on the best available information, data, analysis and scientific expertise and take into account all potential alternative solutions to a problem. If used systematically and as an administration-wide approach, regulatory impact assessment (RIA) provides a critical tool to ensure greater quality of the PA's intervention. (OECD, 2020[15]) The RIA process itself is a systematic approach to weigh the benefits and costs of various regulatory and non-regulatory options for the PA to address a specific problem in society. Governments must make decisions for new laws based on a sound rationale and evidence; otherwise, regulations and policies will not be-fit-for-purpose and, in the worst case, may do more harm than good.

RIA is a fundamental part of the OECD *Recommendation on Regulatory Policy and Governance* [OECD/LEGAL/0390] (see Box 8.1).

Box 8.1. OECD Best Practice Principles for Regulatory Impact Assessment

1. **Commitment and buy in for RIA**
   - Governments should:
     - Spell out what governments consider as "good regulations".
     - Introduce RIA as part of a comprehensive long-term plan to boost the quality of regulation.
     - Create an oversight unit for RIA with sufficient competences.
     - Create credible "internal and external constraints", which guarantee that RIA will effectively be implemented.
     - Secure political backing of RIA.
   - Securing stakeholder support is essential.
   - Governments have to enable public control of the RIA process.

2. **Governance of RIA – having the right set up or system design**
   - RIA should be fully integrated with other regulatory management tools and should be implemented in the context of the Regulatory Governance Cycle.
   - RIA and its implementation should be adjusted to the legal and administrative system and culture of the country.
   - Governments need to decide whether to implement RIA at once or gradually.
   - Responsibilities for RIA programme elements have to be allocated carefully.
   - Efficient regulatory oversight is a crucial precondition for a successful RIA.
   - Resources invested in RIA must be carefully targeted.
   - Parliaments should be encouraged to set up their own procedures to guarantee the quality of legislation, including the quality of RIA.

3. **Embedding RIA through strengthening capacity and accountability of the administration**
   - Adequate training must be provided to civil servants.

- Governments should publish detailed guidance material.
- There should be only limited exceptions to the general rule that RIA is required.
- Accountability- and performance-oriented arrangements should be implemented.

4. Targeted and appropriate RIA methodology

- The RIA methodology should be as simple and flexible as possible, while ensuring certain key features are covered.
- RIA should not always be interpreted as requiring a full-fledged quantitative cost-benefit analysis of legislation.
- Sound strategies on collecting and accessing data must be developed.
- RIA has to be undertaken at the inception stage of policy development.
- No RIA can be successful without defining the policy context and objectives, in particular the systematic identification of the problem.
- All plausible alternatives, including non-regulatory solutions must be taken into account.
- It is essential to always identify all relevant direct and indirect costs as well as benefits.
- Public consultations must be incorporated systematically in the RIA process.
- Insights from behavioural economics should be considered, as appropriate.
- The development of enforcement and compliance strategies should be part of every RIA.
- RIA should be perceived as an iterative process.
- Results of RIA should be well communicated.

5. Continuous monitoring, evaluation and improvement of RIA

- It is important to validate the real impacts of adopted regulations after their implementation.
- RIA systems should also have an in-built monitoring, evaluation and refinement mechanism in place.
- A regular, comprehensive evaluation of the impact of RIA on the (perceived) quality of regulatory decisions is essential.
- It is important to evaluate the impacts in cases where the original RIA document does not coincide with the final text of the proposal.
- Systematic evaluation of the performance of the regulatory oversight bodies is important.

Source: (OECD, 2020[15])

Figure 8.1. Most OECD countries have RIA requirements and implement them in practice

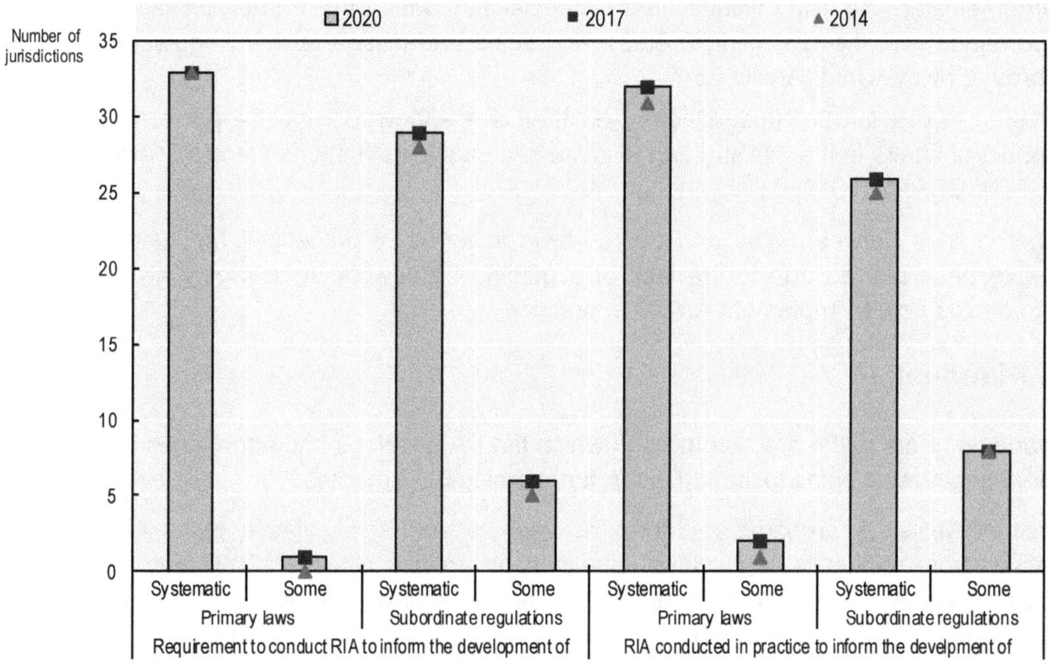

	Requirement to conduct RIA to inform the development of: Primary laws – Systematic	Primary laws – Some	Subordinate regulations – Systematic	Subordinate regulations – Some	RIA conducted in practice to inform the develpment of: Primary laws – Systematic	Primary laws – Some	Subordinate regulations – Systematic	Subordinate regulations – Some

Note: Data are based on 34 OECD Member countries and the European Union.
Source: Indicators of Regulatory Policy and Governance (iREG) Surveys 2014, 2017 and 2021.

OECD Member countries have recognised the importance of regulatory impact assessment. Since 2021, all OECD Member countries have a requirement in place to conduct RIA on at least some laws, and there has also been a slight rebalancing as Members move away from a blanket requirement to a more proportionate approach. The gap between a requirement to conduct RIA and what actually happens in practice is slowly reducing. (OECD, 2021[11])

In line with international best practice, the Palestinian Authority has committed to underpin the development of its regulatory interventions on a number of good regulatory principles, including impact assessment. Those principles are spelled out in the *Legislative Drafting Guidelines* prepared by the Ministry of Justice with the support of the European Union Police Mission for the Palestinian Territories (EUPOL COPPS) and the OECD.

Types of regulatory instruments

In the Palestinian Authority, primary laws are prepared under Regular procedure. In cases of necessity or when the Parliament is not in session, laws are issued by the President as decree laws in an Exceptional procedure. The two types of laws do not have the same legal value (as decree laws in theory will need approval by the Legislative Council once it is again in session), but the distinction between them is not always made. Article 43 decree laws do however have "the power of law" and also the capacity to become "proper" laws provided that the PLC approves them when back in session.

The Council of Ministers has the right (and positive obligation) to initiate primary laws, while the issuance of decree-laws is a discretionary power of the President as per the Basic Law.

The executive can issue the following instruments according to the Basic Law:

- Council of Ministers issues *allawayih* (secondary regulations): the CoM "shall have the right [...] to issue regulations" (Article 70);
- Prime Minister (the 'PM') issues *qararat* (decisions) "within the Prime Minister's competence in accordance with the law" (Article 68.6), and signs and issues *lawa'h* (regulations) and *anthima* approved by the CoM (Article 68.7);
- Ministers issue *ta'limat* (instructions), as they are endowed with the power to "supervise the conduct of affairs in the ministry and to issue necessary instructions therefor" (Article 71.2). (EUPOL COPPS, 2017[1])

In practice, the lines between laws and decree-laws in terms of processes for their preparation and issuance have been blurred due to the lack of a guiding framework. It is largely at the government's discretion to decide how to implement Art. 43 in practice.

Forward Planning

Forward planning refers to the practice through which the PA develops and announces on a regular basis the regulatory initiatives it plans to launch in the forthcoming 6-12 months.

The Council of Ministers prepares mid-term as well as annual legislative plans with support from representatives from ministries' legal units, albeit on an *ad hoc* basis. In 2007 and 2012, the Higher National Committee (HNC) and a Ministerial Committee on Legislative Policies (MCLP) were established in an effort to streamline the process of forward planning, however both committees are currently inactive. (EUPOL COPPS, 2017[1])

The Cabinet Decision no. (06/18/14) of 2012 on the *Approval of the Recommendations of the Ministerial Committee on Legislative Policies* established the mechanism for the preparation and implementation of the annual legislative plan. Ministries were tasked with preparing sectoral legislative plans in consultation with relevant stakeholders and submitting them to the General Secretariat for review. The MCLP was to assess coherence of the ministries and other bodies' plans with overarching policy objectives and submit them to the Council of Ministers.

To date however, there is no formal, harmonised process for forward planning of rule-making activities in practice, though individual departments sometimes engage in independent legislative planning, such as the Ministry for Women's Affairs, which prepares internal strategic and operational plans and objectives. As a result, awareness of administration-wide legislative planning activities is limited.

When administration-wide legislative plans are developed, their implementation is not consistent nor effective. The General Secretariat of the Council of Ministers is tasked with monitoring the implementation of the PA's legislative plan. However, ministries reported that legislation was prepared, with short or no advance notice and weak strategic coherence with the overarching policy agenda.

The legislative process in the Palestinian Authority

The legislative process in the Palestinian Authority is the result of exceptional international and domestic political developments and needs to be reviewed in this context in order to be understood. The absence of the parliamentary body since 2007 had a profound impact on the processes for making primary laws, effectively eliminating the democratic system of control by the legislature.

As a result, there are two different procedures in place for developing legislation in the Palestinian Authority: The regular procedure, applicable when the PLC is in session, and the exceptional procedure during periods when the legislature is absent.

Regular procedure

The PA's regular law-drafting procedure is rooted in the Basic Law, which provides that both the executive and the legislative may initiate primary legislation. In line with the democratic principle of the separation of powers, the Basic Law invested the PLC with the power to adopt laws that are initiated by the executive.

The Basic Law assigns ministries the power to "prepare drafts and legislation related to the ministry and propose them to the Council of Ministers" (Article 71.4). The legislative proposals should be based on the *General Development Plan* prepared by the CoM (see Part I for further information on the procedures for policy development). Sometimes, committees established by the CoM look into certain technical issues to propose a policy response and task the relevant ministry with developing the draft.

The legislative draft is sent to the Diwan, which prepares a formal draft without altering legislative substance or purpose. In its drafting, the Diwan considers the consistency of the proposed legislation with the Basic Law and existing legislation. Once drafted by the Diwan and, if necessary, revised by the promoting ministry, the legislative drafts are sent to the General Secretariat of the Council of Ministers, where they are discussed in three readings and, again, scrutinised for consistency with existing legislation.

The General Secretariat of the Council of Ministers should refer the draft for consideration to a ministerial committee consisting of a number of relevant ministers and the head of the Diwan, under the chairmanship of the Minister of Justice (as set out in *Law No. 4 1995*). If this committee approves the draft, it is returned to the full Council of Ministers, which may accept or reject it, or ask for it to be amended. In practice, such committee is yet to be implemented and the Diwan is currently pursuing its establishment.

If the Council asks for amendments, the draft is returned to the Diwan for revision before being submitted to the Legislative Council. The President shall promulgate the laws voted by the Palestinian Legislative Council within 30 days of reception according to Art. 41 of the Basic Law. The President may refer a law back to the Legislative Council with his observations and the reasons of his objection within the same period. Otherwise, the law will be deemed promulgated and will be published in the Official Gazette. If the President of the PA returns the proposed law to the Legislative Council within the time limit, the Council shall debate the law again. If the Council passes the law a second time, whether in its old or amended form, by a majority of two-thirds of its members, the proposed law shall be considered approved and shall be immediately published in the Official Gazette.

All laws are published by the Diwan in the PA's Official Gazette as per *Law no. (4) 1995 Concerning the Procedures for Preparing Legislation*, and come into effect 30 days after publication. The Gazette can be accessed online via the online legal database Al-Muqtafi managed by Birzeit University. The Diwan also publishes laws and regulations on its website.

Exceptional procedure

Since 2007, the legislative process in the PA takes place in the absence of the Legislative Council. Article 43 of the Basic Law (see Box 8.2) grants the President the power to issue legislation in the form of presidential decrees in cases of necessity and when the Legislative Council is not in session.

Box 8.2. Art.43 of the Basic Law

Art. 43 Basic Law: "The President of the National Authority shall have the right in cases of necessity that cannot be delayed and when the Legislative Council is not in session, to issue decrees that have the power of law. These decrees shall be presented to the Legislative Council in the first session convened after their issuance, otherwise they will cease to have the power of law. If these decrees are presented to the Legislative Council, as mentioned above, but are not approved by the latter, then they shall cease to have the power of law."

Source: (Palestinian National Authority, 2005[16])

In the absence of the Council, the Council of Ministers should submit the revised draft of legislation that requires the President's approval[1] to the President's Legal Adviser (PLA), who submits it for review to the General Administration for Legal Affairs (GALA) and its Department for Legislation. The focus of the review is placed on necessity, assessed also in light of the explanatory memorandum, where it is provided, and financial implications. For subordinate legislation, the draft is submitted to the Prime Minister who has the authority to issue as per Article 68 (7) of the Basic Law.

The absence of the legislature since 2007 raises the question of legitimacy of Palestinian law. Article 43 *de facto* establishes a discretionary power for the President to issue legislation as he sees fit, which is why it is meant to be used sparingly and in exceptional circumstances. Article 47 (3) requires for elections to be held regularly: "elections shall be conducted once every four (4) years in a regular manner". The Basic Law therefore clearly does not foresee a prolonged use of Art. 43. The last elections for the Palestinian Legislative Council were held in 2006. This absence of political legitimacy is criticised by civil society organisations in the PA, and Palestinian scholars argue for the "people (to) be put back at the centre" of the legislative process (Khalil, 2013[16]).

In addition, Article 43 lacks regulation or further specification and it is at the discretion of the executive to decide how decree-laws should be prepared. This leads to inconsistent practices across the administration whereby institutions other than the Council of Ministers, such as the Diwan, sometimes put legislation forward.

In the absence of the PLC, all laws are provisional laws[2] . It is unclear what their status is and will be once elections will take place. According to the Basic Law, "[...] these decrees shall be presented to the Legislative Council in the first session convened after their issuance; otherwise they will cease to have the power of law. If these decrees are presented to the Legislative Council, as mentioned above, but are not approved by the latter, then they shall cease to have the power of law".

Given the amount of legislation the PA produced since 2007 and the fact that Gaza has been also enacting laws, this would require a substantial effort to 1) organise and prioritise the presentation of legislation to the PLC and 2) decide the principles for harmonising WB and Gaza laws.

In addition, many presidential decrees issued as per Art.43 during the absence of the PLC went beyond the criterion of "[...] cases of necessity that cannot be delayed". As a result, two legislative systems have emerged in the West Bank and the Gaza Strip and the PA suffers from a duality and contradictions in legislations in both parts of the territories.

The legislative drafting guidelines (Box 8.3) provide guidance on the drafting process to civil servants in the PA. The guidelines are broadly in line with OECD recommendations and contain a number of good practice provisions, such as the need for defining the policy issue at hand and for assessing different regulatory and non-regulatory alternatives.

Box 8.3. The Legislative Drafting Guidelines

The legislative drafting guid**elines were prepared in 2018 by a working group**[3] **led by the Ministry of Justice** in cooperation with EUPOL COPPS. They were originally approved when prepared by the OECD in 2013 by Prime Minister Rami Hamdallah at the official launching of the two manuals, and build on earlier versions of the guidelines developed in 2000 and evaluated by the OECD in 2011. The legislative drafting guidelines have been approved by the Council of Ministers pursuant to Resolution No. (17/174/07) of 2017 on 10/10/2017 and are considered binding.

Goals of the guidelines:

- Provide a procedural and technical guideline for preparing primary laws and subordinate regulations for competent authorities (legal units in ministries, Advisory and Legislation Bureau, etc.) based on international best practice;
- Unify the methods of preparing legislation in the Palestinian community (West Bank and Gaza).

The guidelines contain two parts, one on the stages of drafting primary legislation and one on the particularities of drafting secondary legislation.

Part one: Stages of drafting primary legislation

- *Planning stage*: Civil servants should specify the problem and planning impact evaluation, and plan the regulatory impact assessment (definition of the problem and SMART[4] goals, identification of regulatory and non-regulatory options incl. the option to do nothing), consultations, enforcement, and evaluation;
- *Legislative Policy*: This section explains the purpose of the "National Policy Agenda" and the process of translating overarching policy priorities into concrete regulatory proposals by preparing a legislative policy memorandum;
- *Action Plan:* Upon receipt of the legislative policy memorandum, the competent authority is tasked with preparing an action plan to prepare the drafting process. This includes assigning tasks among team members, preparing a list of regulatory elements to be drafted, and anticipating enforcement measures;
- *Legislation Unit:* This section explains the structure to be used when drafting a primary law (preamble, definitions, goals, enforcement);
- *Transitional and permanent provisions*: This section refers to different implementation methods for primary laws, which can be transitional ("articles that that pave the way to transition from the implementation of a previous legislation to a new implementation which amends or annuls it") and permanent.
- *Standards of legislative drafting*: This section specifies the language to be used when drafting articles of a primary law.

Part two of the guidelines specifies the particularities of drafting secondary legislation, which mainly refer to the drafting structure of different types (bylaws, ministerial decisions, instructions).

The guidelines also contain a RIA template[5] in the Annex.

Source: (Palestinian Authority Ministry of Justice, 2018[17])

While the guidelines explain in detail the legislative drafting process as such (e.g. the language and structure of primary laws), they lack more detailed explanation of the tools and processes used to assess regulatory impacts. It remains unclear how cost and benefits of a regulatory proposal can be assessed and how relevant data sources can be accessed, for example. The need for anticipating enforcement measures is mentioned, but no further detail is provided on how this can be done. Furthermore, the practical implications of the distinction between transitional and permanent provisions are not clear.

The Diwan currently develops an article that proposes a streamlined legislative process and promotes the use of good regulatory practices by providing bespoke guidance. The article will contain procedural instructions on impact assessment and consultations and will be accompanied by an action plan. Its implementation is foreseen as part of the Diwan's implementation plan for 2021, but is currently at a halt.

Ex ante regulatory impact assessment

Despite the existence of a formal requirement and guidance material, the systematic assessment of regulatory impacts ex ante so far has been lacking in practice in the Palestinian Authority.

Regulatory impact assessment is a fundamental process for ensuring that regulations meet the needs of businesses and people. A consistent, administration-wide approach to the use of RIA helps gather robust evidence when diagnosing the drivers of societal problems, justify the PA's intervention, identify various possible courses of action (both regulatory and non-regulatory), and compare them against their anticipated costs and benefits.

Current procedure

The obligation to conduct RIA according to the legislative drafting guidelines has been in place since 2017, introduced by the Council of Ministers Resolution No. (17/174/07). The resolution states that each legislative draft should accompanied with an explanatory memorandum, a general policy paper, and an impact assessment related to the regulation. According to the Ministry of Justice, presidential decrees are exempted from the requirement to carry out a RIA.

The guidelines provide an overview of the impact assessment process for both primary and secondary legislation, which is broadly in line with the OECD *Best Practice Principles for Regulatory Impact Assessment* (OECD, 2020[15]). They state that:

> *"[A] written policy document [should be prepared for] examining benefits, costs and possible outcomes of legislations or any other government intervention. It aims to secure the quality and efficiency of government intervention."*

The guidelines' emphasis on the importance of considering several regulatory and non-regulatory options, incl. the option to do nothing, follows international best practice and is particularly positive in light of the "regulatory reflex" prevalent in some ministries. However, a step-by-step guide to assessing regulatory costs and benefits is missing.

The RIA template provided in the guidelines is a good starting point for introducing impact assessments in practice, but some key elements are missing. Most notably, the template should include the expected net costs and benefits of the proposal.

In practice, RIA is not yet part of the process of developing new laws and regulations. A simplified impact assessment is carried out only in some parts of the administration and on an *ad hoc* basis. Priority consideration has so far been given to the identification of financial impacts: for some legislative drafts, the Ministry of Finance has been asked to assess financial and budget impacts. Other (distributional) socio-economic impacts are rarely being considered at present in practice, if at all.

Unlike in several OECD countries, there is not an extended or more in-depth RIA required for proposals with more substantial impacts in the PA. Many OECD countries require a simpler level of assessment for decisions with less complexity or limited economic impact. A full RIA is carried out after the preliminary impact assessment suggests that the impacts require a deeper analysis. This approach helps target scarce public resources towards the most burdensome pieces of legislation. See Box 8.4 and Box 8.5 for OECD best practices and country examples in this regard, as well as practice 2 of the accompanying Good Practice Manual.

Box 8.4. Best Practice Principles on RIA: Proportionality

RIA should not always be interpreted as requiring a full-fledged, quantitative cost-benefit analysis of legislation. A full assessment of macroeconomic impacts necessarily requires the adoption of sophisticated economic modelling. It is unlikely to be feasible in the majority of cases, given the general scarcity of expertise and resources available for the conduct of RIA in most countries. In such circumstances, implementing requirements to undertake substantially more demanding analyses involving general equilibrium models risks having perverse impacts, by diverting resources and focus from more feasible RIA tasks. Rather than always engaging in quantitative cost-benefit analysis, it is essential that officials in charge of RIA identify all possible direct and indirect impacts of alternative options that can in principle address and solve the identified policy problem.

For partial or simplified analysis, typically the methodological choices available to administrations are the following:

- **Least cost analysis** looks only at costs, in order to select the alternative option that entails the lowest cost. This method is typically chosen whenever benefits are fixed, and the administrations only needs to choose how to achieve them.
- **Cost-effectiveness analysis (CEA)** entails that administrations quantify (not monetise) the benefits that would be generated by one USD of costs imposed on society. The typical method used to compare options is thus the so-called benefit-cost ratio, which means dividing the benefits by costs. This method is normally used to all expenditure programs, as it leads to identifying the "value for money" of various expenditure programs. A typical question that can be answered through cost-effectiveness analysis is "how many jobs will be created for every Dollar invested in this option?"; or, "how many lives are saved by every Euro spent on this option?".
- **Cost-benefit analysis (CBA)** entails the monetisation of all (or the most important) costs and benefits related to all viable alternatives at hand. In its most recurrent form, it disregards distributional impacts and only focuses on the selection of the regulatory alternative that exhibits the highest societal net benefit. Accordingly, the most common methodology in cost-benefit analysis is the "net benefits" calculation, which differs from the "benefit/cost ratio" method that is typically used in cost-effectiveness analysis (being benefit minus costs, rather than benefits divided by costs).
- **Multi-criteria analysis** allows a comparison of alternative policy options along a set of predetermined criteria. For example, criteria chosen could include the impact on SMEs, the degree of protection of fundamental rights, consumer protection, etc. Multi-Criteria Analysis is particularly useful when Impact Assessment has to be reconciled with specific policy objectives, and as such is used as an instrument of policy coherence. This method is more likely to capture distributional impacts, although this crucially depends on the criteria chosen for evaluating options.

Source: (OECD, 2020[15]), (OECD, 2015[17]).

Box 8.5. Proportionality in RIA: Country examples for quantitative RIA thresholds

Austria: For all new laws and regulations, an impact assessment is mandatory. The regulation underpinning this instrument provides an explicit list of impact dimensions that have to be assessed. Nevertheless, only impacts above a certain threshold have to be assessed in further detail. Thresholds are mostly quantitative and vary depending on the impact dimension, e.g. for environmental impacts it exceeds 10 000 tons of CO2 per year. Other relevant (sub-)dimensions include impacts on the business cycle (threshold 500 enterprises) and financial impacts like impacts on access to finance (threshold 2.5 million € or 10 000 enterprises). As a consequence, only for about 35% of new laws have a full scale RIA and resources can be directed to proposals where high quality impact assessments are needed.

Canada: Canada applies RIA to all subordinate regulations, but employs a Triage System to decide the extent of the analysis. The Triage System underscores the Cabinet Directive on Regulatory Management's principle of proportionally, in order to focus the analysis where it is most needed. The development of a Triage Statement early in the development of the regulatory proposal determines whether the proposal will require a full or expedited RIA, based on costs and other factors.

- Low impact, cost less than 10 million dollars present value over a 10-year period or less than 1 million annually;
- Medium impact: Costs 10 million to 100 million present value or 1 million to 10 million annually;
- High impact: Costs greater than 100 million present value or greater than 10 million annually.

United States: RIA is required for significant and economically significant regulatory actions as defined under Executive Order 128666 and Executive Order 13563. An economically significant regulatory action is one that:

- Likely to impose costs, benefits, or transfers of $100 million or more in any given year;
- Adversely affect in a material way the economy, a sector of the economy, productivity, competition, jobs, the environment, public health or safety, or State, local, or tribal governments or communities.

Source: (OECD, 2019[18])

Because of the still relatively novel character of the tool in the PA, there is the risk for RIA to be seen largely as a mechanistic "tick-the-box" exercise to be deployed after concrete decisions have been made on the political level. There is limited appreciation of the benefits associated with using RIA as a process to facilitate policy integration and proportionate interventions, and rationalising public decision-making.

As a result of the lack of RIA implementation, there is weak understanding among PA officials of how regulatory interventions affect incentives for stakeholders and the public to change behaviour, and of the types of impacts that PA interventions are likely to trigger.

It is not seldom that PA laws have to be reconsidered ("frozen") because of the emergence of unintended consequences, either because the likely impacts had not been anticipated or correctly appraised *ex ante*, or because regulated parties face compliance challenges.

Skills and analytical capacities

As explained in section 3 Capacities, the PA operates with severely strained financial and, most importantly, analytical resources. This particularly affects the approach to regulating and the implementation of regulatory impact assessment in practice, or lack thereof.

Ministries and bodies with key competencies in the regulatory process are understaffed and lack analytical resources. Staff in ministries consists mostly of lawyers and legal specialists. This informs the instinctive approach to regulation by the legal departments, which tend to act upon a “regulatory reflex” without necessarily addressing the drivers of the problem and alternative, non-regulatory interventions in a comprehensive manner. In addition, economists, social scientists, and public policy specialists able to analyse wider social and economic impacts and carry out a comprehensive cost-benefit-analysis are missing. As a result, regulatory impact assessment is yet to be implemented in practice in ministries.

Also, there is a lack of practical guidance available to civil servants in legal departments, as discussed earlier in this section. The legislative drafting guidelines are an important step towards introducing an effective, transparent, and evidence-based approach to legislation making in the Palestinian Authority. At the same time, a more hands-on, practical guide explaining the different steps of legislative drafting and tools such as cost-benefit-analysis in detail is missing. Birzeit University's Institute of Law prepared a regulatory impact assessment guide as part of an EU-funded project on building a sustainable legal aid system in the PA (Birzeit University Institute of Law, 2017[19]), which reiterates the need for RIA but does not provide practical instructions either.

Lastly, there is no targeted training available to civil servants on how to carry out an impact assessment in practice.

Data availability and accessibility

RIA should be supported with clear policies, training programmes, guidance and quality control mechanisms for data collection and use. Where relevant, RIA should make use of existing data and evaluation indicators – e.g., for countries monitoring performance indicators as part of the budget process, those collected by Ministries of Finance and audited by the Supreme Audit Institution. (OECD, 2020[15])

Data availability and quality, an essential element of proper analysis, is one of the most challenging aspects of RIA because it can be time- and resource-consuming to collect adequate data and it requires a systematic and functional approach.

OECD research showed that data availability for the assessment of regulatory impacts is an issue in the PA. A lack of availability of or access to relevant data significantly hampers objective and effective regulatory analyses and evidence-based decision-making. Most ministries reported that the lack of data availability poses an important challenge for collecting, processing, validating and using evidence throughout the phases of formulating policies and elaborating the PA's (regulatory) interventions. Some ministries rely exclusively on indicators and data collected internally.

In addition, existing data is difficult to access due to strict confidentiality rules introduced by the *access to information* law, which hampers ministries' ability to use existing data for decision making. Reportedly, civil servants also do not know where to locate adequate data sources as the legislative drafting guidelines do not contain information on where to find the data needed to support evidence-based regulation making.

Such deficit is both the cause and the consequence of other shortfalls of the PA system: a lack of good quality, easily accessible data contributes to poor policy design and in turn potentially to regulatory failure; exacerbates the dependence on external stakeholders for information; and is linked to a lack of awareness and expertise. (Allio, 2021[20])

Regulatory oversight of impact assessment

Although the Diwan is the *de facto* oversight body, several bodies share oversight functions with regards to regulatory impact assessment. In interviews, the Diwan, the Office of the President, and the General Secretariat of the Council of Ministers reported asking for the explanatory memorandum, should the draft be submitted to them without one. The GS has rejected legislative proposals in the past because the financial impacts were deemed not sufficiently assessed by the Ministry of Finance.

Crucially, there is no body responsible for systematically supporting and controlling the quality of regulatory impact assessment. The Diwan currently takes on the role of a *de facto* ROB, but due to the lack of implementation of RIA in practice this role is limited to requesting the impact assessment statement. In addition, the Diwan is not well positioned for providing support to ministries with RIA in the way the legislative process is currently organised, because it exchanges with ministries too late in the process. The Diwan is often involved in the final stages of the drafting process only, when the legislative proposal is almost final. Due to such oversight functions not being part of Diwan's current mandate, ministries also reportedly do not accept feedback or support provided by the Diwan with regards to impact assessment.

Legal quality

Several bodies share the responsibility for reviewing the legal quality of legislative drafts in the Palestinian Authority. The President's Legal Advisor, the GS of the Council of Ministers, the Diwan, and the Ministry of Justice all scrutinise the consistency with existing legislation and the formal quality of the draft at different stages in the regulatory process. There is also a committee tasked with reviewing consistency with international law and treaties during the legislative drafting process, the Legislation Harmonisation Committee headed by the Ministry of Justice.

All these bodies carry out their review independently. There seems to be no co-ordination of this effort or sharing of best practices. Currently, the Diwan is pursuing an extension of its mandate that will i.a. introduce a legislative quality unit tasked with reviewing legal quality. This move could help consolidate the responsibility for controlling legal quality within one body.

Considering alternatives to regulation

To ensure that the policy solution effectively addresses the problem at hand, it is important to identify and qualify, quantify and possibly monetise several types of impacts of several regulatory and non-regulatory alternatives (including the no-action option). The Good Practice Manual complementing this review discusses the process of identifying possible appropriate instruments in Practice 3.2. *Thinking of regulatory and non-regulatory instruments*.

Following OECD best practice, the legislative drafting guidelines require the proposing ministry to identify at least three different options (Table 8.1): regulatory, non-regulatory, and the do-nothing option. Costs, advantages, and impacts on public spending have to be assessed for all options, including distributional impacts, i.e. the regulatory impacts on different groups in society. The latter is a rather advanced practice that even countries with well-developed regulatory systems have not yet implemented fully.

Table 8.1. Table of options in PA RIA

Option	Costs	Advantages	Impact on public spending	
Option 1				
Option 2				
Option 3				

Source: (Ministry of Justice of the Palestinian Authority, 2018[21])

In practice, ministries do not yet assess alternatives to regulations regularly when proposing new legislation. On the contrary, ministries tend to approach policy issues with a "regulatory reflex", i.e. issuing regulations without first analysing the underlying policy problem and considering non-regulatory alternatives including the option to do nothing.

Recommendations

Mid-term and annual legislative plans are being produced on an ad hoc basis. A formal, harmonised process for forward planning of rule-making activities is still missing with some ministries preparing legislative plans individually. The failure to effectively plan and prioritise legislative and regulatory interventions and the lack of implementation when such plans are in place affects the effectiveness of PA interventions at all levels.

The revision of the legislative drafting guidelines led to notable improvements, bringing them broadly in line with the OECD standards and good international practice. The most important steps of the regulation making process are reflected in the guidelines. Nevertheless, some aspects are unclear and key elements are missing. Notably, there is a need for step-by-step, hands-on guidance on the application of good regulatory practices such as the analysis of regulatory costs and benefits when developing legislation.

There is no formalised approach to the drafting process and roles and responsibilities are unclear and partly overlapping. The process of developing laws in absence of the Parliament is not specified and it is at the discretion of the executive to decide how decree-laws should be prepared. This leads to inconsistent practices across the administration. Tasks that in other countries are typically in the responsibility of line ministries, such as providing rationale for the regulatory intervention or organising public consultations, are sometimes carried out by other bodies such as the Diwan, the Ministry of Justice or the GS, albeit in an un-coordinated and unsystematic manner. There is no consistent approach to legislative drafting *within* ministries either. Often, several departments are involved in the drafting process without co-ordinating with each other. The lack of a formalised approach to the drafting process hampers effective regulation making and policy integration.

Despite a formal requirement, regulatory impact assessment is yet to be carried out in practice. The Legislative Drafting Guidelines are mostly in line with international best practice and are an important step towards establishing a RIA system, yet implementation is lacking behind. This might partly be due the lack of systematic communication within the administration on the benefits of RIA to convey the importance and purpose of such analysis to civil servants. As a result, RIA is considered an additional burdensome obligation with unclear benefits in an already cumbersome legislative process. Most importantly, a lack of analytical capacities in line ministries affects the implementation of regulatory impact assessment in practice.

Data availability and accessibility, essential elements of proper impact analysis, are an issue in the PA. A lack of availability and difficult access to relevant data significantly hampers objective and effective regulatory analyses and evidence-based decision-making. To date, the legislative drafting guidelines do not provide guidance on data collection strategies and adequate sources.

The regulatory impact assessment system is not yet supported by regulatory oversight. There is no body responsible for systematically supporting and controlling the quality of regulatory impact assessment. The Diwan as the *de facto* oversight body requests impact assessment statements from ministries, but gets involved too late in the legislative process to be able to help ministries preparing them.

Recommendation 8.1 - Consider formalising, organising and making systematic the process of forward planning and developing new regulations. Roles and responsibilities of actors involved should be clearly assigned.

- Formalise the legislative drafting guidelines to organise and make systematic the forward planning process, the RIA process, and the intra- and inter-ministerial consultation processes;
- Organise and monitor the development and implementation of the PA's legislative plan by a dedicated body. To this end, the PA should consider re-establishing the Ministerial Committee on

Legislative Policies (MCLP) under the lead of the Ministry of Justice (as already discussed in Recommendation 7.2);

- Cleary assign ministries a (stronger) role in the regulatory process within the guidelines. In OECD countries, functions like carrying out research on the rationale of the draft law and organising stakeholder consultations are typically within the responsibility of the lead ministry. In the PA, the Diwan, the Ministry of Justice, and the General Secretariat of the Council of Ministers currently carry out those functions;
- Clearly communicate roles and responsibilities to all stakeholders across the administration to increase transparency and foster buy-in with the changes occurring in the system of better regulation. The goal should be to establish relationships of "no surprises", whereby entities know who is responsible for each given function and understand clearly the processes and requirements for creating and passing a regulatory proposal into law to minimise frictions and maximise compliance.

Recommendation 8.2 - Introduce ex ante regulatory impact assessment gradually in practice as a default condition for any regulatory proposal.

- Implement and enforce the requirement progressively. Transition phases and adjustment time may be envisaged to allow gradual familiarisation and compliance with the requirement by the ministries. It could be envisaged to "pilot-test" the RIA requirement in one or several ministries over the course of 1-3 years with the support of the OECD. Results of the pilots should be used to inform the existing methodology.
- Introduce a proportional approach to RIA to help target scarce public resources to the most burdensome pieces of legislation:
  - Determine the objective cases when a RIA is a priori not necessary (exclusion criteria) and when a RIA may not be carried out (exemption conditions), and establish the related arrangements to ascertain and manage such cases; exclusions and exceptions should be kept at a minimum and based on clear criteria against which they should be justified (see *Good Practice Manual* Practice 2 for practical guidance on this issue);
  - Ensure a proportionate allocation of time and resources to the elaboration of RIAs, by tailoring the scope and depth of the analyses to the significance and magnitude of the expected impacts. A threshold could be introduced outlining criteria that allow legislation to undergo a simplified RIA process. This effort would have to be supported by the oversight body scrutinising the decision to conduct a simple RIA;
- Create "RIA Working Groups" (or equivalent) to support implementation in practice, and leverage policy integration and structurally sharing multi-disciplinary expertise;
- Revise the RIA template[6] in the legislative drafting guidelines to include key elements such as net costs and benefits of the regulatory proposal;
- Establish that each RIA be signed off by the minister responsible for the proposal, to ensure ownership and accountability;

Recommendation 8.3 - Support the implementation of RIA in practice by putting in place effective regulatory oversight. Quality control of legal quality should be consolidated in one single body and these functions should be granted and regulated by law, in line with the Basic Law.

- Ensure that the regulatory oversight function is carried out by an independent body close to the centre of government. The Diwan, as PA's *de facto* ROB, is well placed to carry out regulatory oversight functions with regards to RIA, including quality control of impact assessments and providing support to ministries. The development of the article expanding Diwan's mandate to include oversight functions should be further pursued. The article will also introduce a new legislative quality unit that would be well placed to carry out review of legal quality which is currently split between Diwan, GS, MoJ, and OoP.

- Ensure that the new oversight function is exercised with flexibility in relation to the type and level of support that the ROB provides to ministries and to the stringency with which draft RIA reports are scrutinised by the ROB. In the beginning, the ROB should focus its oversight function on providing support to ministries tasked with preparing a RIA and promoting the use of the standardised RIA template.
- Provide for the evaluation by the ROB of the whole RIA system for efficiency and effectiveness, once it is running in practice. Performance of individual ministries could be "named and praised" in annual reports to promote compliance.

Recommendation 8.4 - Provide guidance on data collection[7] as part of the legislative drafting guidelines. It should make use of stakeholder input to facilitate the use of reliable and relevant evidence in support of the regulatory process.

- Reference the public sources of data and information that could be used to carry out the corresponding assessment, such as the Palestinian Central Bureau of Statistics in the section on data collection. Complementary data sources must likewise be defined, e.g. surveys or meetings with stakeholder groups;
- Pay particular attention to fully using the potential of stakeholder consultation as a source for data as well as a means to verify its quality. It should be emphasised that in the early consultation stages, there are plenty of possibilities for gathering information, which, ultimately, will allow to conduct a correct assessment of public policy proposals. To this end, it is important that draft RIA reports form part of the documentation put on internal and external public consultation and that they may be commented upon by stakeholders.

References

Allio, L. (2021), "Good Practices Manual. Implementation support for the project "Support the Palestinian Authority to enhance Governance and the Rule of Law". [10]

Birzeit University Institute of Law (2017), *Regulatory Impact Assessment Guide for Legislation and Government Interventions*. [9]

EUPOL COPPS (2017), *The Legislative Process in the Palestinian Authority*. [3]

Khalil, A. (2013), "Beyond the written constitution: Constitutional crisis of, and the institutional deadlock in, the Palestinian political system as entrenched in the basic law", *International Journal of Constitutional Law*, Vol. 11/1, pp. 34-73, https://doi.org/10.1093/ICON/MOS022. [5]

Ministry of Justice of the Palestinian Authority (2018), "The Legislative Drafting Guidelines". [11]

OECD (2021), *OECD Regulatory Policy Outlook 2021*, OECD Publishing, Paris, https://doi.org/10.1787/38b0fdb1-en. [2]

OECD (2020), *Regulatory Impact Assessment*, OECD Best Practice Principles for Regulatory Policy, OECD Publishing, Paris, https://doi.org/10.1787/7a9638cb-en. [1]

OECD (2019), *A closer look at proportionality and threshold tests for RIA*, OECD. [8]

OECD (2015), *Regulatory Policy in Perspective: A Reader's Companion to the OECD Regulatory Policy Outlook 2015*, https://www.oecd.org/gov/regulatory-policy-in-perspective-9789264241800-en.htm (accessed on 26 October 2021). [7]

Palestinian Authority Ministry of Justice (2018), "The Legislative Drafting Guidelines". [6]

Palestinian National Authority (2005), *Basic Law of the Palestinian National Authority*. [4]

Notes

[1] See Types of regulatory instruments for legislation the executive can issue independently.

[2] In December 2018 the Constitutional Court dissolved the PLC. However, decree laws issued after this date still refer to the Basic Law of 2003 and therefore, the obligation to present the laws to the PLC, once elected, remains.

[3] Members of the working group: Office of the President's Legal Unit, the Council of Ministers and its General Secretariat, the Ministries of Interior and Finance, the Advisory and Legislation Bureau (Diwan Alfatwa), Birzeit and Al-Quds Universities, and representatives from the private sector.

[4] SMART = **S**pecific, **M**easurable, **A**greed upon, **R**ealistic, **T**ime specific.

[5] See Annex A Legislative Drafting Guidelines: Palestinian Authority RIA Template

[6] See the UK RIA template as an example in Annex B RIA Template.

[7] Further information and best practices for a more comprehensive data strategy can be found in the OECD Digital government Studies issue *The Path to Becoming a Data-Driven Public Sector*, Chapter 2, and the OECD Digital government Toolkit, Principle 3 *Creation of a Data-Driven Culture in the Public Sector* as well as the Best Practice Principles for RIA (OECD, 2020[15]).

9 Stakeholder Engagement and Transparency

This section reviews the processes in place in the Palestinian Authority for consultation and dialogue with affected stakeholders and the general public and to what extent the outcomes can influence policy makers. It describes and evaluates the regulatory and institutional framework for stakeholder engagement and the role of stakeholder engagement in ex ante and regulatory impact assessment.

The guidelines on public consultation provide a good normative basis for stakeholder engagement in the regulatory process, but there is no formal provision for systematic consultation outside the administration and practical guidance is lacking. Public consultation in the Palestinian Authority takes place on an *ad hoc* basis. The absence of a functioning legislature amplifies the need for stakeholder engagement and transparency in the legislative process. This section therefore recommends that the PA make public consultation a requirement and systematically publish draft legislation online for comment.

Transparency is one of the central pillars of effective regulation, supporting accountability, sustaining confidence in the legal environment, making regulations more secure and accessible, less influenced by special interests, and therefore more open to competition, trade and investment.

The central objective of regulatory policy – ensuring that regulations are designed and implemented in the public interest – can only be achieved with help from those interested in and affected by regulations – the "stakeholders". Stakeholders should not only be consulted when new regulation is being proposed and developed, they should also have an opportunity to participate in subsequent phases of the "regulatory governance cycle", such as regulatory delivery or reviewing the regulatory stock.

According to the *OECD Recommendation on Regulatory Policy and Governance* [OECD/LEGAL/0390], "governments should establish a clear policy identifying how open and balanced public consultation on the development of rules will take place". Governments should be actively engaging all relevant stakeholders during the regulation-making process and designing consultation processes to maximise the quality of the information received and its effectiveness (see Box 9.1).

Box 9.1. OECD Recommendation on Regulatory Policy and Governance: Stakeholder Engagement

1. Governments should establish a **clear policy** identifying how open and balanced public consultation on the development of rules will take place.
2. Governments should **co-operate with stakeholders on reviewing existing and developing new regulations** by:

- Actively engaging all relevant stakeholders during the regulation-making process and designing consultation processes to maximise the quality of the information received and its effectiveness.
- Consulting on all aspects of impact assessment analysis and using, for example, impact assessments as part of the consultation process;
- Making available to the public, as far as possible, all relevant material from regulatory dossiers including the supporting analyses, and the reasons for regulatory decisions as well as all relevant data;
- Structuring reviews of regulations around the needs of those affected by regulation, co-operating with them through the design and conduct of reviews including prioritisation, assessment of regulations and drafting simplification proposals;
- Evaluating the competitive effects of regulation on various economic players in the market.

3. Introduce regular **performance assessments of regulations** and regulatory systems, taking into account, among other things, the impacts on affected parties and how they are perceived. Communicate the results of these assessments to the public.
4. Make sure that policies and practices for **inspections and enforcement respect the legitimate rights of those subject to the enforcement,** are designed to maximise the net public benefits through compliance and enforcement and avoid unnecessary burdens on those subject to inspections.

5. All regulations should be **easily accessible** by the public. A complete and up-to-date legislative and regulatory database should be freely available to the public in a searchable format through a user-friendly interface over the Internet.
6. Governments should have a policy that requires regulatory texts to be **drafted using plain language.** They should also provide clear guidance on compliance with regulations, making sure that affected parties understand their rights and obligations.

Source: (OECD, 2012[5])

All OECD countries are making use of some form of stakeholder engagement during the regulatory process, albeit at different stages of the regulatory policy cycle and with different forms of consultations (OECD, 2021[11]).

Similarly to OECD countries, the Palestinian Authority is carrying out efforts to engage stakeholders in the rule-making process. However, public consultation takes place against the backdrop of an extremely complicated political and legal environment. In the absence of a functioning legislature, public consultation to inform draft legislation is of particular importance. This need is amplified by the unspecific nature of Art. 43 in the Basic Law that allows for "many pieces of legislation [being issued], mostly uninformed, unjustifiable, and in certain cases unconstitutional" (Birzeit University, Institute of Law 2010, cited in (OECD, 2011[9])).

There is no formal provision for systematic consultation outside the administration to be carried out on draft legislation. The public consultation guidelines aim to provide a practical framework civil servants can turn to when tasked with preparing legislation. In 2018, the Ministry of Justice issued Guidelines on Public Consultations, which were prepared by a working group[1] and based on the *OECD Practitioner's Guide for Engaging Stakeholders* (OECD, 2011[9]) (see Box 9.2).

Box 9.2. The Guidelines on Public Consultation

The **Guidelines on Public Consultation** were issued by the Ministry of Justice in 2018 and prepared by a working group consisting of the legal unit at the PO, the CoM, several ministries, private sector representatives, and universities, with the support of EUPOL COPPS. They build on the OECD Manual on regulatory consultation in the PA (OECD, 2011[6]).

The Guidelines aim at institutionalising consultation on draft legislation with the public and introduced information on desired institutional set-up for carrying out public consultation, as well as timeframes, stages, tools and usage of results.

The Guidelines outline different stages for organising public consultations:

1. *Legislative policy stage (preliminary stage):* At the preliminary stage, central aspects of the consultation process should be determined (Why is there a need for consultation? Who will organise the consultation? Who should be consulted? What is the timeline? Which tools should be used? What are the required resources?). The creation of a working group/dedicated committee is advised.
2. *Implementation stage (during implementation):* At this stage, the parties affected by the legislation should be consulted with, making use of a range of tools (public meetings, online consultation, working groups with selected stakeholders, phone calls, surveys).
3. *Evaluation stage (final stage):* Feedback received during the consultation process should be documented in feedback tables and should be responded to. A control mechanism to oversee

the process of consultations should be put in place to provide feedback on the quality of the consultation process.

The guidelines are set to be evaluated and, if necessary, revised two years after implementation.

Source: (Palestinian Authority Ministry of Justice, 2018[23])

The guidelines are an important step towards establishing an inclusive and transparent legislative process and broadly follow OECD best practice principles for engaging stakeholders in the regulatory process. They contain some crucial steps of successful engagement, such as the importance of advance planning and responding to stakeholder feedback.

Nevertheless, some important elements are missing. Crucially, there is no formal requirement by law to carry out stakeholder engagement. The guidelines strongly encourage ministries to follow the outlined procedures, but they are not considered legally binding.

Also, a minimum period for public consultation has not been specified in the guidelines. The time needed to carry out consultations remains at the ministries' discretion. While the OECD does not recommend a specific minimum period, many countries require or recommend minimum periods of 30 or 60 days for stakeholders to have sufficient time to submit their views (or longer, when the regulatory proposal is particularly complex) (OECD, forthcoming[22]).

Regarding timeframes set for public consultations, the guidelines recommend planning ahead and allowing for sufficient time to engage, in line with international best practice. They however also make mention of consultation under "exceptional circumstances", which should be carried out "briefly". The exceptional circumstances are not further defined, but it can be assumed that the guidelines refer to legislation making under Art. 43 of the Basic Law. As a result, civil servants consulting the guidelines could get the impression that stakeholder engagement in the current legislative system is negligible.

The guidelines list a number of tools that can be used for carrying out public consultations. A more detailed explanation on how those tools can be used and what steps need to be taken is however missing. Selecting the right tools is an important step in planning stakeholder engagement activities and depends on a variety of factors, notably the objectives of the project, stakeholders participating, and available resources. Civil servants will therefore need detailed information to be able to assess which tool is appropriate to use under the given circumstances. Such information can be found in Practice 5 of the *Good Practice Manual*.

Most importantly, a clear, detailed, and hands-on guide on different tools and techniques that can be used to engage stakeholders in the regulation making process is missing. The guidelines provide a good normative framework for consultation practices in the PA, but remain relatively vague and high-level. Civil servants will need step-by-step, practical guidance including examples and templates for the different tools and techniques available to consult with stakeholders.

In practice, public consultation in the PA takes place on an ad hoc basis, as discussed in the following section.

Early stage consultations

Governments should consult with all significantly affected and potentially interested parties, where appropriate, at the earliest possible stage while developing regulations (OECD, 2020[15]). When involving stakeholders early in the policy cycle – at the stage before the preferred solution has been identified and the paragraph wording drafted, and at the stage when the administration is still able and willing to significantly change the regulatory draft – governments can achieve much better effects and improve regulatory outcomes.

In the Palestinian Authority, there is no explicit and binding requirement to engage with external stakeholders at the early stage of the regulatory process, i.e. when the solution has not yet been identified. In practice, consultation with the public at the early stage is rarely carried out, if at all. The impetus to legislate reportedly does not come from consultations with affected stakeholders, but rather from ad hoc political requests to produce a certain kind of legislation.

Late stage consultations

Stakeholder engagement at the later stage, i.e. when the regulatory solution has been identified, is not mandatory in the Palestinian Authority. In practice, it is carried out on *ad hoc* basis and primarily for drafts prepared by a Council of Ministers committee. There is no systematic approach to consulting with stakeholders outside of the administration to inform the development of draft legislation.

According to the consultation guidelines, teams within ministries headed by the Ministry deputy or representative are responsible for organising and carrying out consultations. This is in line with OECD recommendations, which state that the institution responsible for drafting or reviewing regulations in their area of competence should also be responsible for engaging stakeholders in the drafting/review process.

Yet, in practice, the General Secretariat of the Council of Ministers and the Ministry of Justice usually organise the consultations on behalf of ministries. The General Secretariat is also present at every consultation. Draft legislation is not yet published online for consultation, and "public" consultation is currently limited to surveys and workshops with selected stakeholders.

The consultation takes place shortly before it is submitted to the Council of Ministers. At this stage, the draft is already very advanced. In a first step, the GS initiates correspondence with stakeholders, usually CSOs or other structures in the community. The Council of Ministers issues official letters to consult them on the draft. Depending on the issue at hand, the GS sometimes also organises stakeholder workshops, for example to discuss amendments to the recently issued local administration law. A series of workshops was organised that included all entities, officials and otherwise affected stakeholders.

In cases where there are complaints by stakeholders on the content of a draft law, the President's Office puts in place *ad hoc* committees to discuss the stakeholder's concerns and reach to a consensus.

Crucially, draft legislation is not yet made available online for public consultation. Publishing draft legislation for comments helps to reach a broader and more diverse range of stakeholders to provide their input than working groups and surveys with selected groups only. See Box 9.3 for examples of online consultation portals used by EU Member States.

Box 9.3. Selected consultation portals in EU Member States

Austria: Since September 2017, all draft primary laws are available on the website of Parliament together with a short description of the legislative project in accessible language, the RIA and other accompanying documents. The public can submit comments on the draft regulation or support comments made by others online.

Croatia: On the interactive consultation portal e-Savjetovanja, major draft regulations are published for consultation for a minimum of 30 days. The website allows the public to provide general feedback on the draft or to provide comments on the individual articles of a draft regulation. The comments are publicly displayed alongside the draft, allowing other members of the public or policy makers to react. For major draft primary laws, RIA statements are also made available for comments.

Slovak Republic: Public consultations are required for every legislative proposal submitted to the Slovak government. All legislative drafts and their accompanying impact assessments are automatically published on the government portal www.slov-lex.sk at the same time as they enter the inter-ministerial comment procedure. The portal provides a single access point to comment on legislative proposals and non-legislative drafts (e.g. concept notes, green or white papers).

Source: (OECD, 2019[23])

Information and comments provided are collected in a table prepared by the Ministry of Justice. The template for the table as included in the consultation guidelines requires civil servants carrying out the consultation to respond to the comments received and to justify how the feedback has been taken into account. In practice, this is rarely, if ever, the case. The table is then sent to the CoM and the Diwan prepares the final draft of the legislation.

There is little evidence that comments received lead to changes in the draft. Private sector representatives reported that their feedback rarely leads to changes in the draft law. Also, the "freezing" of legislation shortly after issuance occurs on a regular basis, partly due to conflicts with affected stakeholders that had not been consulted with sufficiently during the development stage.

Transparency and e-government

By adhering to international conventions, the Palestinian Authority has committed to principles of transparency, such as "open government", which includes the right of people to access information, financial transparency, transparency in governance and policymaking, and guaranteeing the protection of public freedoms.

The need for transparency in the regulatory process and consultations with stakeholders to inform draft legislation is exacerbated by the inactivity of the parliamentary body in the PA. Stakeholders external to the administration can, to a certain extent, fill the gap of checks and balances created by the absence of Parliament and can provide and verify data and information used to inform the decision making process.

The PA undertakes some efforts to introduce transparency in the regulatory process. All laws and regulations are published on the *Electronic Reference for the Official Gazette* web portal managed by the Diwan[2], as well as the Al-Muqtafi platform[3], a legal data bank managed by Birzeit University's Institute of Law. Al-Muqtafi contains all legislation since the Ottoman period and is continuously updated and upgraded. Most recently, Al Najah University has initiated an electronic legal platform. All websites are run in parallel with no coordination between the Diwan and the universities to align their efforts. The OECD helped strengthen these online tools in the framework of an EU-funded project on rule of law and governance. Capacity-building activities aimed at enhancing online access to legislation by supporting the standardised production of visual and social media content, the improvement of digital tools to access draft legislation and a greater coordination with key institutional and non- institutional stakeholders.

Currently, there is no administration-wide platform or portal where draft legislation is published for public consultation, even though the guidelines recommend such practice. The websites run by Diwan and Birzeit University are used to publish final laws and regulations only. Some ministries, like the Ministry of Social Development, publish draft legislation on their own website for public consultation. The MoSD also consults with unions and coordination councils on these laws.The Ministry of Communications and Information Technology launched an online portal "My Government" in 2018 in cooperation with the Land Authority, the Ministry of Labor, and the Ministry of Transport. While the portal provides public services such as getting land permits and access to public documents, it so far has not allowed for people to consult or provide feedback on draft or existing legislation.

The PA's latest effort to improve transparency in the regulatory process and make use of e-government tools is the *e-hub* portal currently under development by the Council of Ministers. The purpose of the portal is to publish the PA's legislative plan, serve as a communication tool between the ministries and the CoM, and provide an open channel for complaints and suggestions concerning existing legislation from the public. The *e-hub* project does not yet foresee a public consultation feature to inform the development of draft legislation.

Regulatory oversight of consultations

Governments should create mechanisms ensuring that civil servants adhere to the principles of open government and stakeholder engagement in regulatory policy, including through efficient oversight.

The consultation guidelines assign this responsibility to the ministry carrying out the consultation. They state that "(...) oversight on public consultations can be done at the department with the team that is charged with preparing legislation. This oversight is exercised through a minister or his deputy, by participating in team meetings from time to time, and through periodic reports received from the team." In addition, the guidelines mention the Office of the President and the Ministry of Justice as responsible for overseeing the quality of the engagement process. According to OECD best practice, regulatory oversight and quality control of the consultation process should be carried out by a body independent from the ministry responsible for conducting the consultation.

There is currently no regulatory oversight of the quality of stakeholder consultations, yet a number of bodies are involved in the consultation process. The GS of the CoM participates in ministries' interactions with stakeholders and the Diwan receives all stakeholder engagement reports. The Ministry of Justice sometimes organises consultations on behalf of ministries and prepares the feedback table.

The current involvement of the GS and the Diwan makes the two bodies well-placed to carry out such function in the future.

Recommendations

The consultation guidelines are an important step towards more inclusive and transparent decision making. They are broadly in line with OECD best practice for stakeholder engagement and contain many good practices for consultation, such as setting clear timelines in advance and replying to comments received. Nevertheless, some important elements are missing. Notably, there is no minimum period for consultations outlined in the guidelines. The time needed to carry out public consultation remains at the ministries' discretion.

Consultation with the public to inform legislative drafts is currently carried out sporadically, and the effectiveness and impact of the consultations carried out is unclear. As draft legislation is not published for consultation, people and businesses impacted by the legislation are often denied the opportunity to provide feedback during the development stage. At the same time, private sector representatives reported that their feedback provided in workshops organised by the PA rarely leads to changes in the draft law. The lack of systematic stakeholder engagement exposes government to undue influence in setting the regulatory agenda and providing information, and represents a missed opportunity for gathering evidence.

There is no systematic approach to stakeholder engagement in regulation making and roles and responsibilities for stakeholder engagement and organising consultations as laid out in the guidelines are not being followed. A number of bodies carry out functions that should be in the responsibility of line ministries, albeit not in a co-ordinated fashion. Notably, both the General Secretariat and the Ministry of Justice sometimes organise consultations on behalf of ministries. The President's Office establishes working groups to discuss stakeholder's concerns on draft legislation in parallel to those efforts and outcomes are not always shared. The absence of a consistent and formalised approach to stakeholder engagement leads to insufficient involvement of people and businesses in regulation making. As a result, policy makers forego the opportunity to collect valuable evidence needed to make informed decisions.

The PA makes use of a number of online tools to introduce transparency in the legislative process. Notably, the Council of Ministers currently develops an *e-hub* portal to publish the annual legislative plan and provide an open channel for complaints to the public. The Diwan and Birzeit University both publish laws featured in the Gazette on their respective websites. This effort is however not carried out in a co-ordinated manner and draft legislation is not published. Even though recommended by the consultation guidelines, there is currently no online portal for publishing draft legislation.

A regulatory oversight mechanism to ensure that stakeholder engagement activities are in line with the consultation guidelines is yet to be introduced. While several bodies are involved in the stakeholder engagement process, such as the Ministry of Justice and the GS of the CoM, there is no body tasked with overseeing if and how consultations are carried out and supporting ministries if needed. The guidelines assign the ministries carrying out the consultation the responsibility to review the quality, however according to OECD experience this task should be carried out by a body independent to the one conducting the stakeholder engagement to ensure un-biased quality control.

Recommendation 9.1 - Pursue and intensify its commitment to a participatory, inclusive and responsive decision-making process by making the consultation of the public a general requirement for all regulatory interventions, promoting the use of a variety of tools and channels of public engagement, and setting binding minimum consultation standards.

- Make the public consultation guidelines legally binding by resolution, introducing a formal provision to carry out consultation for all legislative interventions. In addition, the requirement to carry out public consultation should be clearly stated as part of the article to better organise the legislative process currently under development by the Diwan. It should also be part of the whole-of-government strategy in Recommendation 6.1.;
- Include within the guidelines a minimum period for consultations for stakeholders to have sufficient time to submit their views. While the OECD does not recommend a specific minimum period, many countries require or recommend minimum periods of 30 or 60 days (or longer, when the regulatory proposal is particularly complex);
- Help PA civil servants in designing a consultation process suiting the regulatory issue at hand, which can differ greatly in impact and importance, scope and number of affected groups, information needs, timing of public action and resources available for consultation. To this end, guidelines and training efforts should inform about and promote the use of a variety of tools and channels of public engagement as discussed in the *Good Practice Manual* (Practices 3 and 5).

Recommendation 9.2 - Ensure a transparent and user-friendly access to information by developing, consolidating, and upgrading the features of the PA web-portals, creating a pivotal platform for both public consultation and communication. Draft legislation should be published for public consultation.

- Systematically publish draft legislation online and in a user-friendly manner, with clear instructions for the public on how to provide comments - *a key strategic policy objective under National Policy 9 in the "National Policy Agenda"*.
- Issue and publish "Notices of Government Intervention" online to inform internal and external stakeholders of the main regulatory and non-regulatory forms of a planned public intervention (see accompanying *Good Practice Manual*).
- Consider enhancing the operational coordination between Diwan and relevant academic institutions (e.g. Birzeit University, Al Najah University, etc.) regarding their respective web portals. Currently, the websites are used to publish existing legislation. Strengthened coordination could help to ensure that contents complement and do not contradict each other. With the extension of the Diwan's mandate, the Bureau could take the lead in this effort as well as the responsibility for publishing draft legislation for consultation with the public, creating a pivotal platform for both public consultation and communication.
- Should Diwan's new mandate not allow for this new role, publish legislative drafts on the forthcoming *e-hub* portal currently under development by the Council of Ministers. The portal should include a comment feature, allowing the administration and the public to view and respond to comments received. This practice fosters stakeholders' trust in public institutions and can help alleviate consultation fatigue.

Recommendation 9.3 - Support the implementation of the consultation guidelines and sure enforcement by a body outside of the ministry carrying out the consultation.

- Consolidate the quality control function of regulatory management tools – regulatory impact assessment, stakeholder engagement, and ex post evaluation –in one single body outside the ministry sponsoring the draft legislation. The Diwan would be well positioned to take on the oversight function for stakeholder engagement, potentially supported by the GS of the CoM, who is heavily involved in the public consultation process and participates in all stakeholder consultation meetings and workshops.

References

OECD (2021), *OECD Regulatory Policy Outlook 2021*, OECD Publishing, Paris, https://doi.org/10.1787/38b0fdb1-en. [2]

OECD (2020), *Regulatory Impact Assessment*, OECD Best Practice Principles for Regulatory Policy, OECD Publishing, Paris, https://doi.org/10.1787/7a9638cb-en. [6]

OECD (2019), *Better Regulation Practices across the European Union*, OECD, http://GOV/RPC(2018)15/REV1. [7]

OECD (2012), *Recommendation of the Council on Regulatory Policy and Governance*, https://legalinstruments.oecd.org/en/instruments/OECD-LEGAL-0390 (accessed on 7 November 2018). [1]

OECD (2011), *Regulatory Consultation in the Palestinian Authority*, https://www.oecd.org/mena/governance/50402841.pdf (accessed on 26 March 2021). [3]

OECD (forthcoming), *OECD Best Practice Principles on Regulatory Policy: Stakeholder Engagement*, OECD Publishing, Paris. [5]

Palestinian Authority Ministry of Justice (2018), "Guidelines on Public Consultation". [4]

Notes

[1] Ministry of Justice, Legal Unit of the PO, Council of Ministers, Ministry of Interior, Advisory and Legislation Bureau, the GS of the Council of Ministers, Palestinian Bar Association, Private Sector representatives, Birzeit University, Al-Quds University, Ministry of Finance and Planning.

[2] https://mjr.lab.pna.ps/.

[3] http://muqtafi.birzeit.edu.

10 Management of the Existing Stock of Regulations

This section examines whether the Palestinian Authority has put in place processes for monitoring and reviewing the existing stock of regulations and laws, including how it undertakes reforms to improve regulation in specific areas or sectors to reduce administrative burdens or evaluate the overall effectiveness of regulation.

The statute book is uniquely complex and fragmented, containing laws issued under different regimes dating back to the era of the Ottoman Empire. This in turn means that is difficult for regulated subjects to understand and navigate existing rules. This section therefore recommends that policies and mechanisms need to be established to ensure that this stock of legislation undergoes some form of ex post reviews over time, to ensure that it remains fit for purpose.

The existing body of law has been issued under several political regimes (see Chapter 1 "Political Context"). The law is a blend of Islamic customary law, *Urf*, and the principles of Islamic *Shari'a* (the main source of legislation), the stock of legislation applied or enacted under the Ottoman Empire (1516-1917), British Mandate Law (1917-1948), Jordanian legislation applied to the West Bank and Egyptian legislation applied to the Gaza Strip (1948-1967) and, of course, legislation enacted by the Palestinian Authority since 1994. This legacy creates a significant challenge when drafting new legislation. In addition, the political split between Gaza and the West Bank with the different legal traditions has far-reaching implications for the legislative process and impedes consolidation efforts for the Palestinian legal system. (OECD, 2011[9])

The PA has not yet put in place a comprehensive set of policies and mechanisms to ensure that the existing laws and regulations on the statute book will be monitored and reviewed as to their effectiveness. There are occasional, limited, elements of *ex post* review requirements in its current legislative drafting and consultation guidelines, and some forms of *ex post* evaluation are being implemented by certain line ministries on an *ad hoc* basis (Ministry of Justice of the Palestinian Authority, 2018[21]). However, *ex post* evaluation does not take place systematically across line ministries, and civil servants lack guidance and methodologies, as well as sufficient training, to carry such reviews out.

Ex post evaluation

OECD best practice suggests that regulations should be periodically reviewed to ensure that they remain fit for purpose. Regulations that are efficient today may become inefficient tomorrow, due to social, economic, or technological change. Most OECD countries have enormous stocks of regulation and administrative formalities that have accumulated over years or decades without adequate review and revision. The accumulated costs of this in economic or social terms can be high.

Ex post evaluations complete the "regulatory cycle" that begins with *ex ante* assessment of proposals and proceeds to implementation and administration. The importance of using *ex post* evaluations to assess the ongoing worth of regulations is recognised in the OECD Recommendation on Regulatory Policy and Governance [OECD/LEGAL/0390] (see Box 10.1). It states that Member governments should *"conduct systematic reviews of the stock of regulation … to ensure that regulations remain up to date, ... cost effective and consistent, and deliver the intended policy objectives"* [OECD/LEGAL/0390].

Box 10.1. The fifth recommendation of the Council on Regulatory Policy and Governance

Conduct systematic programme reviews of the stock of significant regulation against clearly defined policy goals, including consideration of costs and benefits, to ensure that regulations remain up to date, cost justified, cost-effective and consistent and delivers the intended policy objectives.

- The methods of Regulatory Impact Analysis should be integrated in programmes for the review and revision of existing regulations. These programmes should include an explicit objective to improve the efficiency and effectiveness of the regulations, including better design of regulatory instruments and to lessen regulatory costs for citizens and businesses as part of a policy to promote economic efficiency.
- Reviews should preferably be scheduled to assess all significant regulation systematically over time, enhance consistency and coherence of the regulatory stock, and reduce unnecessary regulatory burdens and ensure that significant potential unintended consequences of regulation are identified. Priority should be given to identifying ineffective regulation and regulation with significant economic impacts on users and/or impact on risk management. The use of a permanent review mechanism should be considered for inclusion in rules, such as through review clauses in primary laws and sunsetting of subordinate legislation.
- Systems for reviews should assess progress toward achieving coherence with economic, social and environmental policies.
- Programmes of administrative simplification should include measurements of the aggregate burdens of regulation where feasible and consider the use of explicit targets as a means to lessen administrative burdens for citizens and businesses. Qualitative methods should complement the quantitative methods to better target efforts.
- Employ the opportunities of information technology and one-stop shops for licences, permits, and other procedural requirements to make service delivery more streamlined and user-focused.
- Review the means by which citizens and businesses are required to interact with government to satisfy regulatory requirements and reduce transaction costs.

Source (OECD, 2012[5])

The OECD has defined three overarching principles for instituting *ex post* evaluation with public administrations (OECD, 2020[24]):

- Regulatory policy frameworks should explicitly incorporate ex post evaluations as an integral and permanent part of the regulatory cycle;
- A sound system for the ex post evaluation of regulation would ensure comprehensive coverage of the regulatory stock over time while "quality controlling" key reviews and monitoring the system's operations as a whole; and
- Reviews should include an evidence-based assessment of the actual outcomes from regulations against their rationales and objectives, note any lessons and make recommendations to address any performance deficiencies.

However, based on the Indicators of Regulatory Policy and Governance surveys, systems for the *ex post* evaluation of regulation remain less developed across OECD Member countries than for other components of the regulatory cycle, particularly *ex ante* RIA, with fewer countries having formalised arrangements. For example, some form of *ex post* evaluation was recorded as obligatory by only 60% of Member countries, compared to around 90% for *ex ante* RIA (OECD, 2020[24]).

Figure 10.1. Requirements to conduct RIA and ex post evaluation

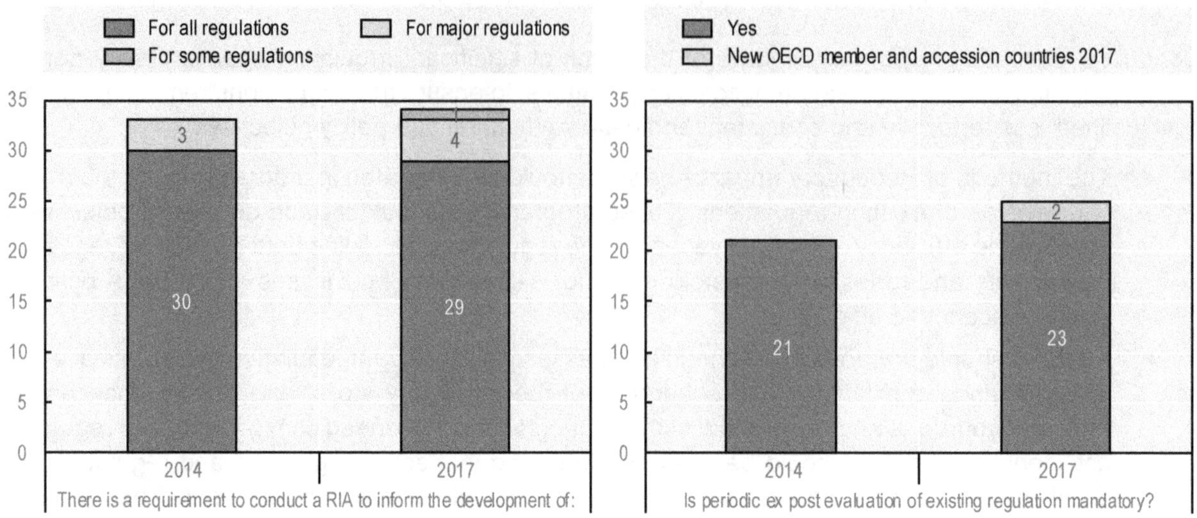

Note: Data for OECD countries is based on the 34 countries that were OECD Member countries in 2014 and the European Union. Data on new OECD Member and accession countries 2017 includes Colombia, Costa Rica, Latvia and Lithuania.
Source: Indicators of Regulatory Policy and Governance Surveys 2014 and 2017, http://oe.cd/ireg.

A "portfolio" of approaches to the *ex post* evaluation of regulation will generally be needed (see Box 10.2). Most countries have adopted more than one of these approaches utilising forms of review within each category listed below, which draw upon a taxonomy developed by the Australian Productivity Commission. Practical ways to embed *ex post* evaluation in a country's policy system include sunset clauses to require governments to review a regulation a certain amount of time after it has been promulgated, scheduled reviews that look at whole policy frameworks for different areas and specialised standing bodies that have a mandate to review regulations and to make recommendations for improvement.

Box 10.2. Approaches to regulatory reviews

A "portfolio" of approaches to the *ex post* evaluation of regulation will generally be needed. In broad terms, such approaches range from programmed reviews, to reviews initiated on an ad hoc basis, or as part of ongoing "management" processes. Most countries have adopted more than one of these approaches utilising forms of review within each category listed below, which draw upon a taxonomy developed by the Australian Productivity Commission.

"Programmed" reviews

- For regulations or laws with potentially important impacts on society or the economy, particularly those containing innovative features or where their effectiveness is uncertain, it is desirable to embed review requirements in the legislative/regulatory framework itself.
- Sunset requirements provide a useful "failsafe" mechanism to ensure the entire stock of subordinate regulation remains fit for purpose over time.
- Post-implementation reviews within a shorter timeframe (1 to 2 years) are relevant to situations in which an ex ante regulatory assessment was deemed inadequate (by an oversight body for example) or a regulation was introduced despite known deficiencies or downside risks.

Ad hoc reviews

- Public "stocktakes" of regulation provide a periodic opportunity to identify current problem areas in specific sectors or the economy as a whole.
- Stocktake-type reviews can also employ a screening criterion or principle to focus on specific performance issues or impacts of concern.
- "In depth" public reviews are appropriate for major regulatory regimes that involve significant complexities or interactions, or that are highly contentious, or both.
- "Benchmarking" of regulation can be a useful mechanism for identifying improvements based on comparisons with jurisdictions having similar policy frameworks and objectives.

Ongoing stock management

- There need to be mechanisms in place that enable "on the ground" learnings within enforcement bodies about a regulation's performance to be conveyed as a matter of course to areas of government with policy responsibility.
- Regulatory offset rules (such as one-in one-out) and Burden Reduction Targets or quotas need to include a requirement that regulations slated for removal, if still "active", first undergo some form of assessment as to their worth.
- Review methods should themselves be reviewed periodically to ensure that they too remain fit for purpose.

Source: (OECD, 2020[24])

The review of the regulatory stock as part of the ex post review process is particularly important since it can help reduce administrative burdens for citizens and businesses as well as improve public sector efficiency. Countries can use a checklist to decide whether certain regulations should be kept, scrapped or modified. Such a checklist was used for example in Croatia (see Box 10.3) and a template was developed by the OECD to provide countries with guidance in developing and implementing better regulation (see Box 10.4).

Box 10.3. Regulatory guillotine in Croatia

To improve the regulatory environment in Croatia, a short-term statute law revision (regulatory guillotine) project, known by its Croatian acronym as HITROREZ, was launched in 2006. The Government initiative co-founded by USAID and UNDP aimed at counting, reviewing and streamlining business regulations in Croatia.

The regulatory guillotine was conducted in the following phases:

- First, the government asked all ministries and agencies to prepare inventory lists of their regulations by a certain date. Each administrative body in co-operation with stakeholders from the private sector prepared a complete list of all regulations with an impact on businesses and people and submitted the list to the Special Unit of HITROREZ together with all associated forms. The process was overseen by a central body.
- Then, Government authorities reviewed each business regulation and its associated forms and fees based on standardised criteria and a questionnaire. Each business regulation was assessed with a recommended action: keep, change or cancel. Those identified as unnecessary, outdated or illegal were excluded from the list.

The special Unit for HITROREZ reviewed each business regulation taking into account feedback from government authorities and the business community, as well as comments from consultations with other relevant stakeholders. The Unit developed final recommendations and presented it to the government of Croatia. As a result, 27% of business regulations were eliminated and 30% were simplified.

Source: (OECD, 2019[25])

Box 10.4. 1995 OECD Recommendation on Improving the Quality of Government Regulation

In 1995, the OECD adopted the Recommendation on Improving the Quality of Government Regulation [OECD/LEGAL/0278] to improve the effectiveness and efficiency of government regulation by upgrading the legal and factual basis for regulations, clarifying options, assisting officials in reaching better decisions, establishing more orderly and predictable decision processes, identifying existing regulations that are outdated or unnecessary, and making government actions more transparent. In order to provide guidance for countries in developing and implementing better regulation, a Reference Checklist for Regulatory Decision-making was issued containing the following ten questions:

Q1. Is the problem correctly defined?

Q2. Is government action justified?

Q3. Is regulation the best form of government action?

Q4. Is there a legal basis for regulation?

Q5. What is the appropriate level (or levels) of government for this action?

Q6. Do the benefits of regulation justify the costs?

Q7. Is the distribution of effects across society transparent?

Q8. Is the regulation clear, consistent, comprehensible, and accessible to users?

Q9. Have all interested parties had the opportunity to present their views?

Q10. How will compliance be achieved?

Source: (OECD, 1995[26])

Current procedures

The PA has placed consolidating the body of law as one of its strategic policy objectives. Under Pillar 1 of the "National Policy Agenda 2017-22: Putting Citizens First" (also see the sub-section "Vision for Regulatory Policy"), the PA has committed to consolidating and modernising PA's body of law to ensure consistency with international obligations (Pillar 1, National Policy 3). The document states:

> *"Our national unity will be further advanced by establishing a modern, coherent body of law reflecting our international commitments and replacing the unwieldy mix of Palestinian, Jordanian, Egyptian and Ottoman laws that derives from colonisation and occupation."*

However, the PA has not yet put in place strong formal requirements or guidance material to ensure that *ex post* evaluations are systematically carried out by line ministries. The **legislative drafting guidelines** (see 6.5), introduced by the Council of Ministers Resolution No. (17/174/07), state that a key step in the legislative process is *"follow-up and evaluation: the party responsible for oversight must evaluate the outcomes and compare them with performance indicators to determine the extent of success of the solution mechanisms in addressing the problem and resolving it.*

Box 10.5. The Legislative Drafting Guidelines – *ex post* evaluation

The legislative drafting guidelines were prepared in 2018 by a working group led by the Ministry of Justice in cooperation with EUPOL COPPS. They build on earlier versions of the guidelines developed in 2000 and evaluated by the OECD in 2011. The legislative drafting guidelines have been approved by the Council of Ministers pursuant to Resolution No. (17/174/07) of 2017 on 10/10/2017 and are considered binding.

Part One:

- Follow up and evaluation: To enable us to know the extent of the correct action taken to solve the problem, the party responsible for oversight must evaluate the outcomes and compare them with performance indicators to determine the extent of success of the solution mechanisms in addressing the problem and resolving it. This however, requires compliance with certain criteria that identify the points of strength and weakness in the legislation after implementing it and determining the procedures that should be reconsidered. The following are among the mechanisms that contribute to the performance of an accurate evaluation:
  - Preparation of periodical reports.
  - Field visits.
  - Obtaining the points of view of the members of the community.
  - Preparation of statistics and comparing them with previous statistics to determine if there is an increase or decrease in same.
  - Monitor the performance indicators and finding out extent of same.
- To achieve a successful follow-up and accurate evaluation, we have to determine in advance during the preparation of the document the parties responsible for this, the monitoring fields, who will do the monitoring and the implementation mechanism.

Source: (Ministry of Justice of the Palestinian Authority, 2018[21])

In addition, the **Guidelines on Public Consultation** (see Box 9.2 in chapter 9**)** issued by the Ministry of Justice in 2018, stipulate that evaluation is a key stage in the public consultation process:

> *"Evaluation process: this process starts after preparing and issuing the legislation it includes follow-up, evaluation, monitoring, and revision of the drafted law after implementation. The process is initiated to measure the law's success in arriving at the targets it was set to facilitate."*

The OECD were informed that there is a complaints department within the OoP that deals with stakeholder complaints about existing legislation. In addition, the OECD were made aware of a number of ad-hoc initiatives for reviewing legislation, undertaken by different parts of the PA.[1] The focus of these reviews have mainly been on addressing any shortcomings and inconsistencies within the legislation or harmonising the legislation with international standards, as opposed a detailed evaluation of the impacts of the legislation. For example:

- The Ministry of Transport have stated that regulations are reviewed in order to remove ambiguity or to harmonise the system, especially since certain regulations have become incompatible with international standards. For example, a regulation contained a provision with names of degrees of driving licenses, which had become incompatible with international classifications. This led to the amendment of the regulation in order to be compatible with those classifications.

- The Diwan have stated that a review has been conducted on legislation related to women. The review examined the legislation from a number of lenses, including social, economic, educational, competitiveness, rights and obligations, and recommendations were made to the Cabinet, to amend some legislation and introduce new legislation.

There have been some initiatives from the PA to introduce e-government services, with the aim of reducing administrative burdens on people. As mentioned in the previous Section "Transparency and e-government", some ministries, the Ministry of Communications and Information Technology in 2018 launched an online portal called "My Government" in cooperation with the Land Authority, the Ministry of Labour, and the Ministry of Transport and Communications.

However, despite the existence of these strategic policy objectives and high-level requirements, in practice, *ex post* evaluation is not yet systematically carried out on existing laws and regulations. There is not currently an explicit policy and guidelines for *ex post* evaluation in place, clearly assigning roles and responsibilities of the actors involved in the review process, or a clear set of requirements for ministries to carry out *ex post* evaluations for existing regulations in the Palestinian Authority .

There is also an absence of a specific methodology for *ex post* review, to assist with identifying priorities for reviews and identifying and measuring the impacts of regulation, including administrative burdens and wider costs and benefit to the economy, society and the environment. Reviews are presently carried out on an *ad hoc* basis according to the modalities of the particular regulation in question. This is very important as there are a number of different approaches that can be taken to institutionalise *ex post* evaluation within an administration's policy process (see Box 10.6). It should be noted that the forthcoming OECD Good Practices Manual for the Palestinian Authority will provide selected practical guidance on how regulatory management tools can be implemented, although detailed methodological guidance will still be required (OECD, forthcoming).

Practical ways to embed *ex post* evaluation in a country's policy system include sunset clauses to require governments to review a regulation a certain amount of time after it has been promulgated. For regulations or laws with potentially important impacts on society or the economy, particularly those containing innovative features or where their effectiveness is uncertain, it is desirable to embed review requirements in the legislative/regulatory framework itself. A selection of international examples of how these approaches have been embedded into government's rule making processes is included in Box 10.6.

Box 10.6. International examples of approaches to *ex post* evaluation

New Zealand

In New Zealand, the Public Service Act stipulates five public service principles. One of them is "stewardship", which explicitly includes within its scope the stewardship of all legislation administered within the public service. This "regulatory stewardship" responsibility views regulation (regulatory systems) as a set of national assets that require proactive monitoring, care and maintenance to deliver effectively over time.

Good regulatory stewardship practice includes:

- Monitoring the performance and the state of the regulatory systems and of the regulatory environment, assessing the regulatory system and evaluating whether it is suitable for the regulatory objective and reporting on regulatory systems
- Systematic assessment of risks and impacts of regulations prior to any changes and enabling interested parties to contribute to the design of regulations
- Providing information and support to regulated parties
- Providing training to regulatory personnel.

European Commission

The European Commission's "evaluate first" principle is a key aspect of its regulatory framework. The "evaluate first" principle calls for the review of regulations before any new proposal is made in an area concerned by the foreseen regulation and that timely and relevant recommendations are given to regulators to support their decision-making. In addition, the evaluation of regulations aids the decision-making process by contributing to the design of future policies.

Source: (OECD, 2021[27])

Furthermore, there has been little attempt to date by the PA to evaluate and reduce the administrative burdens caused by the stock of regulation, despite the aforementioned attempts to introduce e-government initiatives. It appears to be particularly difficult and time consuming for external stakeholders (e.g. Small and Medium Sized Enterprises and people) to understand and navigate existing rules.

OECD best practice points to a range of initiatives that have been undertaken internationally to implement administrative simplification strategies, including attempts to quantify regulatory burdens to businesses and people through well understood methodologies such as the Standard Cost Model (SCM). Governments have also attempted to introduce more 'bottom-up' approaches to understanding regulatory burdens through working closely with stakeholders to identify issues of most concern to them (see Box 10.7). One-stop shops have also been introduced to many OECD countries part of broader administrative simplification strategies.[2]

Box 10.7. International examples of administrative burden reduction

The **Netherlands** carried out a study comparing regulatory burden for SME's in the bakery sector across selected EU Member States. The evaluation compared the impact of the regulatory frameworks in the Netherlands, Lithuania, Spain and Ireland. The objective was to assess whether significant differences existed in the implementation of national and EU legislation resulting in unnecessary regulatory burdens. The review concluded that the use of exemptions and lighter-touch regulatory regimes for SME bakeries in EU laws could reduce regulatory burdens and improve their economic viability.

In **Denmark**, the Ministry for Business and Growth launched the Danish Business Forum in 2012 to identify and discuss the compliance and administrative burden that businesses face. The members of the forum include industry and labour organisations, businesses, as well as experts with expertise in simplification. The forum gathers 3 times a year and sends common proposals to the government on the possible avenues for regulatory simplification. These proposals are subject to a "comply or explain" approach whereby the government is obliged to either pursue the proposed initiatives or to explain why these are not pursued. As of 2016, 603 proposals had been made by the forum of which 191 were fully and 189 partially implemented. The total savings to businesses from the implementation of these simplification measures were estimated to amount to 790 million Danish crowns.

In **Germany**, The Federal Statistical Office was commissioned by the Federal government in 2015 to conduct surveys of individuals and companies on their subjective perception of public authorities and the body of law **in specific life events**. The survey exercise aims to identify measures for a more noticeable bureaucracy reduction and will be repeated every two years. The approach identified typical life events in which citizens people and companies interact with public authorities. 22 life events for individuals were selected ranging from the birth of a child to marriage, unemployment and need for long-term care. Similarly, 10 events for companies based on a company's life cycle were selected, including business start-up, the appointment of employees, and business discontinuation. For every life event, an interactive customer-journey map was constructed displaying the typical and most important offices citizens or businesses have to contact and the procedures they have to complete to obtain the respective service.

Source: (OECD, 2020[24]), (OECD, 2016[28])

Analytical capacities for ex post evaluation

The challenge facing ministries due to understaffing and a lack of analytical resourcing has already been highlighted earlier in the report (see Section 3 "Capacities"). It logically follows that the same capacity challenges clearly exist for successfully implementing *ex post* evaluation. There is a lack of expertise in staff able to analyse wider social and economic impacts and carry out cost-benefit-analysis. There is also a lack of practical guidance available to civil servants, explaining the different tools and approaches to carrying out ex post evaluations. Furthermore, there are no training programmes available to civil servants on how to carry out *ex post* evaluations in practice. Box 10.8 provides some examples of building capacity and providing support to evaluators in OECD countries.

Box 10.8. Building capacity and providing support to evaluators

In **Canada**, the Treasury Board of Canada Secretariat (TBS) Regulatory Affairs Sector initiated a number of measures to assist in building evaluation skills across federal departments and agencies, including:

- the development of a core curriculum by the Canada School of Public Service, which features also a course on "Regulatory performance measurement and evaluation";
- the creation of the Centre of Regulatory Expertise (CORE), which provides technical support concerning cost-benefit analysis, risk assessment, performance measurement and evaluation of regulations; and
- the establishment of the Centre of Excellence for Evaluation (CEE), which serves as a help-desk body in the planning and implementation of evaluations. This includes supporting the competent departments and agencies in the implementation and utilisation of evaluations, and helping to promote the further development of evaluation practices, not least through guidelines and manuals.

In the **European Commission**, in the framework of the Smart Regulation strategy, central support and co-ordination is ensured by the Secretariat-General. The latter issues guidance; provides in-house training; and organises dedicated workshops and seminars. The Secretariat-General oversees the EC's evaluation activities and results and promotes, monitors and reports on good evaluation practice. Evaluation units are present in almost all Directorates-General. Several "evaluation networks" dedicated to specific policy areas are also at work (for instance in relation to research policy or regional policy).

Also in **Switzerland**, despite the fact that there is no central control body for the implementation and support of evaluation in the federal administration, experiences and expertise is shared thanks to an informal "evaluation network". The network exists since 1995 and is directed at all persons interested in evaluation questions, and comprises around 120 members from various institutions.

Source: (OECD, 2018[29])

Data availability and accessibility

Earlier in this report, the difficulties facing the PA regarding data availability for the assessment of regulatory impacts were discussed (see sub-section "Data availability and accessibility") A lack of, availability of or access to relevant data significantly hampers objective and effective regulatory analyses and evidence-based decision-making.

OECD best practice states that data requirements for *ex post* evaluation are best considered at the time a regulation is being made, as part of wider consideration of the type of evaluation that would be most appropriate. Evaluations can fail to produce credible findings and recommendations for lack of adequate "evidence". Standard data collections within the administration may not have the granularity or specificity needed to evaluate all relevant impacts of a regulation. (OECD, 2020[24])

Regulatory oversight

There is no body responsible for systematically supporting and controlling the quality of *ex post* evaluations, which is the same challenge facing RIA (see sub-section "Regulatory oversight of impact assessment"). OECD best practice states that there needs to be oversight and accountability systems within public administrations to provide ongoing assurance that significant areas of regulation will not be missed and that reviews are conducted appropriately. If regulatory agencies and their ministries are left entirely to their own devices, there is a risk that important areas of regulation will not be reviewed, or that reviews will sometimes occur too late (in response to a mishap or "crisis") or that they will not be conducted sufficiently.

In addition, successful international best practice points to benefits in institutional arrangements that combine oversight of the processes for *ex ante* as well as *ex post* assessment. In particular, there is a connection between *ex ante* and *ex post* evaluations, with the former setting up the latter and *ex post* reviews being conducted in the light of *ex ante* assessments, as well as helping to inform further evaluations of new or amended regulation (see Box 10.9).

Box 10.9. Examples linking *ex ante* and *ex post* regulatory oversight in OECD Member countries

Austria has established the system of "Wirkungsorientierte Folgenabschätzung", which introduces systematic requirements for both ex ante and ex post assessments, and requires major regulations to be evaluated after five years. The Federal Performance Management Office is responsible for ensuring the quality of both *ex ante* and *ex post* assessments. In its 2017 report, a regulatory proposal relating to Funding Alpine Infrastructure was highlighted as it explicitly stated that in order to assess the regulation's actual success, impact-orientated data would be required that would allow for progress to be accurately measured. The evidence base would then be expected to form the basis of the ex post evaluation when the regulation was due for review.

The Regulatory Scrutiny Board of the **European Commission** conducts reviews of *ex ante* impact assessments, as well as selected *ex post* evaluations. Its 2017 annual report analysed how impact assessments and ex post evaluations were assessed when regulatory proposals were subject to an informal "upstream meeting" early in the review process with staff of the Commission's services. It generally found that the final impact assessment result had improved where upstream meetings took place – which also tended to be in more complex regulatory areas. The same could not be said for *ex post* evaluations and it was queried whether the limited impact was due to the upstream meeting taking place too late in the evaluation process.

Source: (OECD, 2020[24])

Recommendations

The PA has not yet put in place strong formal requirements or guidance material to ensure that ex post evaluations are systematically carried out by line ministries. This is despite the fact PA has set out a strategic policy objective to consolidate and modernise its statute book in the "National Policy Agenda 2017-22". The PA has also included references to monitoring and evaluation in the legislative drafting guidelines. However, as with *ex ante* RIA, roles and responsibilities of the different actors who would be involved in the review process have not been clearly assigned. There is also no clarity as to when a review should be carried out.

The PA does not have a specific methodology for ex post evaluation. As a result, there is no systematic approach to *ex post* evaluation across the administration. Presently, any reviews are generally carried out on an *ad hoc* basis by line ministries, on a regulation by regulation basis, although the Diwan has informed the OECD that they have carried out a thematic review examining legislation relating to women. Line ministries do not have any guidance as to the different approaches for selecting areas of regulation for review, or how to use different tools (e.g. Cost-Benefit Analysis) to help them understand the impacts of regulations to businesses and society.

There has not been a significant effort to implement administrative simplification strategies. There have been some welcome approaches at implementing e-government initiatives, such as the "My government" online portal. However, PA has an exceptionally complex and fragmented statute book, containing laws issued under different regimes. It is also facing the unique challenge of the political split between Gaza and the West Bank, whereby the two authorities do not enact legislative acts issued by the other. This in turn means that is difficult for external stakeholders (e.g. Small and Medium Sized Enterprises and people) to understand and navigate existing rules. Consolidating and simplifying the statute book will be an ongoing, long term effort across the administration. There are numerous examples internationally of OECD Member countries who have undertaken such efforts. An international example of codification has included Greece, which has been carrying out several reforms of its regulatory framework, including the establishment of a long-term codification plan of the main regulations in 2016 and creation of an electronic portal for the access to regulations as well as simplification of law in selected areas (labour law, VAT) in 2015. (OECD, 2018[12])

A regulatory oversight mechanism to ensure that evaluations are actually carried out, and to a certain quality standard, has yet to be introduced. Ex ante RIA is facing the same challenge (see sub-section "Regulatory oversight of impact assessment"). OECD best practice suggests that there are benefits in institutional arrangements that combine oversight of the processes for *ex ante* as well as *ex post* assessment.

The PA faces significant difficulties regarding data availability for the assessment of regulatory impacts. A lack of availability to relevant data significantly hampers objective and effective regulatory analyses and evidence-based decision-making. There is also potential for greater coherence between *ex ante* RIA and *ex post* evaluation requirements. OECD Best Practice states that *ex ante* RIAs should establish monitoring indicators and data gathering to enable *ex post* evaluation to take place (OECD, 2020[15]).

Recommendation 10.1 - Engage with stakeholders to identify the most burdensome areas of existing legislation.

- Identify the sectors of the economy and society with the most burdensome regulations. Such an exercise would also help generate some momentum behind simplifying the stock of regulations. It should focus *ex post* evaluation efforts on priority areas, which is crucial as OECD experience has shown that the "Pareto principle" can be applied to regulatory burdens – 20% of regulations usually cause 80% of the administrative burden. (OECD, 2010[30]). The PA could run a series of workshops to identify together with stakeholders major policy areas and sectors with the corresponding ministries. This will later enable the PA to implement pilot in-depth reviews of these problematic areas of regulation (see Recommendation 5.2). Beyond looking at regulations in isolation, regular review of regulations and policy measures in key policy areas and sectors that are identified to be of particular economic or social importance can have very high returns.
- Draw upon the e-hub portal currently under development by the Council of Ministers (see the section "Transparency and e-government" to support the identification of the most salient regulatory burdens. This portal could provide an open channel for complaints and suggestions concerning existing legislation from the public.
- Ensure the coordination and monitoring of the programme's implementation by the General Secretariat of the Council of Ministers. However, line ministries should also have a prominent role in running the programmes of engagement with their key stakeholders, for the respective areas of regulation they oversee.

Recommendation 10.2 - Develop a methodology and guidance for ex post evaluation of existing legislation and run pilot tests with ministries.

- Prepare a comprehensive and clear guidance and methodology for ex post evaluations. This methodology should introduce a requirement to assess laws and regulations sometime after their implementation to ensure they meet their objectives. It should clarify when an ex post evaluation needs to be carried out (e.g. x number of years after a regulation is published), as well as the processes to be followed and the different tools that ministries can employ to assess impacts. The different types of ex post evaluation are set out in Box 10.2. The new methodology should be tested through a series of pilots, focused upon the areas of the economy identified in Recommendation 5.1. These pilots should further be supported by clear guidelines.
- Train staff in ministries to conduct evaluations or ensure the quality of evaluations contracted out to academics and to use evaluations of existing regulations before amending regulations. All evaluations should be published online in a central place that is easily accessible to the general public. Resources for evaluation could be focused on high-impact regulations to avoid evaluation fatigue.
- Establish *ex post* evaluation working groups could be established containing representatives from the key line ministries, as well as Diwan, to support implementation of the new methodology in practice, for initiatives of significant importance, and leverage policy integration and structurally sharing multi-disciplinary expertise.
- Ensure the coordination and monitoring of the programme's implementation by the General Secretariat of the Council of Ministers. The Secretariat could co-ordinate *ex post* evaluation efforts to identify priority areas for review together with stakeholders within and outside the administration. In a first step, the body could support ministries in evaluating key policy areas.
- Designate a new oversight body, possibly the Diwan as PA's *de facto* ROB, to carry out quality control of *ex post* evaluations, in addition to *ex ante* RIAs.

Recommendation 10.3 - Carry out a comprehensive review of the stock of regulations.

- Prepare a long term plan with the aim of consolidating and simplifying the exceptionally complex and fragmented Palestinian statute book - *a key strategic policy objective under Pillar 1, National Policy 3 of the "National Policy Agenda 2017-22".* The plan could look to undertake a process of consolidation or codification of the statute book, with a view to achieving clearer language, increased capacity for compliance amongst the regulated population. An example of such an attempt to improve the regulatory environment can be seen in Croatia, where until the early 2000s, the public administration had almost no experience with assessing the consequences of its actions on businesses and people. The first attempt to improve the regulatory environment in Croatia followed in 2006 with the regulatory guillotine project HITROREZ (see Box 10.3).
- Ensure the coordination and monitoring of the programme's implementation, as a cross-administration initiative, by the General Secretariat of the Council of Ministers. However, it will be critical to the success of the programme that line ministries have ownership in their areas of regulation.
- Ask line ministries to compile a database of the existing regulations within each of their respective areas of policy as a starting point. Following this, ministries can undertake a relatively simple exercise by scrutinising their databases of regulation and utilise a set of simple questions or checklist to decide whether certain regulations should be kept, scrapped or modified.

References

Ministry of Justice of the Palestinian Authority (2018), "The Legislative Drafting Guidelines". [2]

OECD (2021), *OECD Regulatory Policy Outlook 2021*, OECD Publishing, Paris, https://doi.org/10.1787/38b0fdb1-en. [7]

OECD (2020), *One-Stop Shops for Citizens and Business*, OECD Best Practice Principles for Regulatory Policy, OECD Publishing, Paris, https://doi.org/10.1787/b0b0924e-en. [13]

OECD (2020), *Regulatory Impact Assessment*, OECD Best Practice Principles for Regulatory Policy, OECD Publishing, Paris, https://doi.org/10.1787/7a9638cb-en. [11]

OECD (2020), *Reviewing the Stock of Regulation*, OECD Best Practice Principles for Regulatory Policy, OECD Publishing, Paris, https://doi.org/10.1787/1a8f33bc-en. [4]

OECD (2019), *Regulatory Policy in Croatia: Implementation is Key*, OECD Reviews of Regulatory Reform, OECD Publishing, Paris, https://doi.org/10.1787/b1c44413-en. [5]

OECD (2018), *OECD Regulatory Policy Outlook 2018*, OECD Publishing, Paris, https://doi.org/10.1787/9789264303072-en. [10]

OECD (2018), *Regulatory Policy in Slovenia: Oversight Matters*, OECD Reviews of Regulatory Reform, OECD Publishing, Paris, https://doi.org/10.1787/9789264291690-en. [9]

OECD (2016), *Pilot database on stakeholder engagement practices in regulatory policy, First set of practice examples*, OECD Publishing, Paris, https://www.oecd.org/gov/regulatory-policy/pilot-database-on-stakeholder-engagement-practices.htm. [8]

OECD (2012), *Recommendation of the Council on Regulatory Policy and Governance*, https://legalinstruments.oecd.org/en/instruments/OECD-LEGAL-0390 (accessed on 7 November 2018). [3]

OECD (2011), *Regulatory Consultation in the Palestinian Authority*, https://www.oecd.org/mena/governance/50402841.pdf (accessed on 26 March 2021). [1]

OECD (2010), *Why Is Administrative Simplification So Complicated?: Looking beyond 2010*, Cutting Red Tape, OECD Publishing, Paris, https://doi.org/10.1787/9789264089754-en. [12]

OECD (1995), *Recommendation of the Council on Improving the Quality of Government Regulation*, OECD Publishing, Paris, https://legalinstruments.oecd.org/en/instruments/OECD-LEGAL-0278. [6]

Notes

[1] This information regarding examples of types of reviews was provided to the OECD by the PA in response to a questionnaire on regulatory policy.

[2] For more information on one-stop shops, see the OECD Best Practice Principles for One- Stop Shops for Citizens and Business. (OECD, 2020[40])

11 Regulatory compliance and enforcement

This section provides a brief overview of the issue of regulatory compliance and enforcement in the Palestinian Authority as an integral part of regulatory policy.

Though beyond the scope of Part II, the issue of regulatory compliance and enforcement is an integral part of regulatory policy and should be mentioned briefly.

As elaborated earlier in Part II, the PA law is a complex blend of regulations issued under several political regimes, dating as far back as the Ottoman Empire, and has been amended several times by different regimes. This "fragmentation of the laws", paired with low public confidence in the judiciary, poses strong challenges for implementing and enforcing laws. Regulatory compliance and enforcement is a significant challenge in the PA. The "freezing" of existing legislation happens on a frequent basis due to compliance issues. More generally, there is a substantial number of laws and regulations that is reportedly simply not being enforced.

This lack of regulatory compliance and enforcement creates significant issues for governance and the rule of law in the PA and should be subject to a more in-depth review. Box 11.1 provides an overview of best practices countries can employ to promote effective and efficient regulatory enforcement.

Box 11.1. OECD Best Practice Principles for Regulatory Policy: Regulatory Enforcement and Inspections

1. **Evidence-based enforcement.** Regulatory enforcement and inspections should be evidence-based and measurement-based: deciding what to inspect and how should be grounded on data and evidence, and results should be evaluated regularly.
2. **Selectivity**. Promoting compliance and enforcing rules should be left to market forces, private sector and civil society actions wherever possible: inspections and enforcement cannot be everywhere and address everything, and there are many other ways to achieve regulations' objectives.
3. **Risk focus and proportionality**. Enforcement needs to be risk-based and proportionate: the frequency of inspections and the resources employed should be proportional to the level of risk and enforcement actions should be aiming at reducing the actual risk posed by infractions.
4. **Responsive regulation**. Enforcement should be based on "responsive regulation" principles: inspection enforcement actions should be modulated depending on the profile and behaviour of specific businesses.
5. **Long term vision**. Governments should adopt policies on regulatory enforcement and inspections: clear objectives should be set and institutional mechanisms set up with clear objectives and a long-term road-map.
6. **Co-ordination and consolidation**. Inspection functions should be co-ordinated and, where needed, consolidated: less duplication and overlaps will ensure better use of public resources, minimise burden on regulated subjects, and maximise effectiveness.
7. **Transparent governance**. Governance structures and human resources policies for regulatory enforcement should support transparency, professionalism, and results oriented management. Execution of regulatory enforcement should be independent from political influence, and compliance promotion efforts should be rewarded.
8. **Information integration**. Information and communication technologies should be used to maximise risk-focus, co-ordination and information-sharing – as well as optimal use of resources.
9. **Clear and fair process**. Governments should ensure clarity of rules and process for enforcement and inspections: coherent legislation to organise inspections and enforcement needs to be adopted and published, and clearly articulate rights and obligations of officials and of businesses.

10. **Compliance promotion.** Transparency and compliance should be promoted through the use of appropriate instruments such as guidance, toolkits and checklists.
11. **Professionalism**. Inspectors should be trained and managed to ensure professionalism, integrity, consistency and transparency: this requires substantial training focusing not only on technical but also on generic inspection skills, and official guidelines for inspectors to help ensure consistency and fairness.

Source: (OECD, 2014[31])

Reference

OECD (2014), *OECD Best Practice Principles for Regulatory Enforcement and Inspections*, https://doi.org/10.1787/9789264208117-en. (accessed on 25 October 2021). [1]

Annex A. Legislative Drafting Guidelines: Palestinian Authority RIA Template

Table A.1. Palestinian Authority RIA Template

Template of the Elements of the Document	
Element	Content
1. Document title on the cover	
2. Executive summary	Includes main elements of the document and outcomes in brief
3. Problem	Focuses on and clarifies main problem and should include the following: • Problem date • Problem causes • Relevant laws • Statistics • Risk assessment • government's position
4. Alternatives	The following must be specified: • Non-action option • Non-legitimate intervention • Legislative-intervention • Legislative and non-legislative intervention For each alternative, the following points need to be examined: • What is the alternative? • Possible impacts • Distribution of impacts, what categories are directly affected by each impact • Financial costs and advantages of the intervention
5. Alternative adopted by the government	One alternative must be selected
6. Public consultations	Parties consulted must be included: • Party consulted • Topic of the consultation • Means of consultation
7. Commitment and implementation	Mention mechanisms and means for implementation and commitment; how mechanism to be implemented and costs of implementation
8. Follow-up and evaluation	Mention follow-up mechanism that will be included in the law (Who control what? When and how?)
9. Recommendation	Mention the important recommendations

Annex B. RIA Template for Government Policies in the United Kingdom

Title: **IA No:** **RPC Reference No:** **Lead department or agency:** **Other departments or agencies:**	Impact Assessment (IA) **Date: 01/01/2020** **Stage: Development/Options** **Source of intervention: Domestic** **Type of measure: Primary legislation** **Contact for enquiries:**
Summary: Intervention and Options	**RPC Opinion:** RPC Opinion Status

Cost of Preferred (or more likely) Option (in 2019 prices)			
Total Net Present Social Value £m	**Business Net Present Value** £m	**Net cost to business per year** £m	**Business Impact Target Status** Qualifying provision

What is the problem under consideration? Why is government action or intervention necessary?

- What is the issue being addressed?
- What are the current or future harms that is being tackled?
- Why is government best placed to resolve the issue?

Maximum of 7 lines

What are the policy objectives of the action or intervention and the intended effects?

- What are the intended outcomes of intervention?
- [optional] Can these be described in a specific, measurable, achievable, realistic and time-limited (SMART), or similar, way?
- What are the desired effects – what will change as a result of intervention?
- What will the indicators of success be?

Maximum of 7 lines

What policy options have been considered, including any alternatives to regulation? Please justify preferred option (further details in Evidence Base)

- Include a description of the "do nothing" option and non-regulatory options.

Maximum of 10 lines

Will the policy be reviewed? It **will/will not** be reviewed. **If applicable, set review date: Month/Year**

Is this measure likely to impact on international trade and investment?		Yes / No		
Are any of these organisations in scope?	**Micro** Yes/No	**Small** Yes/No	**Medium** Yes/No	**Large** Yes/No
What is the CO_2 equivalent change in greenhouse gas emissions? (Million tonnes CO_2 equivalent)		**Traded:**	**Non-traded:**	

I have read the Impact Assessment and I am satisfied that, given the available evidence, it represents a reasonable view of the likely costs, benefits and impact of the leading options.

Signed by the responsible SELECT SIGNATORY: ______________________ Date: ______________________

Summary: Analysis & Evidence

Policy Option 1

Description:

FULL ECONOMIC ASSESSMENT

Price Base Year 2019	PV Base Year 2020	Time Period Years	Net Benefit (Present Value (PV)) (£m)		
			Low: Optional	High: Optional	Best Estimate:

COSTS (£m)	Total Transition (Constant Price)	Years	Average Annual (excl. Transition) (Constant Price)	Total Cost (Present Value)
Low	Optional		Optional	**Optional**
High	Optional		Optional	**Optional**
Best Estimate				

Description and scale of key monetised costs by 'main affected groups'

Maximum of 5 lines

Other key non-monetised costs by 'main affected groups'

Maximum of 5 lines

BENEFITS (£m)	Total Transition (Constant Price)	Years	Average Annual (excl. Transition) (Constant Price)	Total Benefit (Present Value)
Low	Optional		Optional	**Optional**
High	Optional		Optional	**Optional**
Best Estimate				

Description and scale of key monetised benefits by 'main affected groups'

Maximum of 5 lines

Other key non-monetised benefits by 'main affected groups'

Maximum of 5 lines

Key assumptions/sensitivities/risks	Discount rate (%)	

Maximum of 5 lines

BUSINESS ASSESSMENT (Option 1)

Direct impact on business (Equivalent Annual) £m:			Score for Business Impact Target (qualifying provisions only) £m:
Costs:	Benefits:	Net:	

Source: https://assets.publishing.service.gov.uk/government/uploads/system/uploads/attachment_data/file/951405/impact-assessment-template_.docx

www.ingramcontent.com/pod-product-compliance
Lightning Source LLC
LaVergne TN
LVHW081409110826
845149LV00010B/1681

9789264651364